JAMIE'S JOURNEY
An Early American Adventure

by

Vera M. Kierstead

Vera M. Kierstead

Dear Jewel;
You should recognize these family names.
Best wishes

Jan. 22, 2000

1999
"Happy Birthday!"
Love Pat

DORRANCE PUBLISHING CO., INC.
PITTSBURGH, PENNSYLVANIA 15222

ISBN # 0-8059-4615-2
Printed in the United States of America

First Printing

For information or to order additional books, please write:
Dorrance Publishing Co., Inc.
643 Smithfield Street
Pittsburgh, Pennsylvania 15222
U.S.A.

Dedication

To my family,
especially Elisabeth
and Elisabeth Ann,
for their inspiration
and encouragement.

Contents

West By Wagon

"Mrs Allen, should I take this oil painting?" Jamie asked.

"Of course, dear, it is the one your mother asked you to always keep, isn't it?" Mrs. Allen asked.

"Yes, I promised her I would always take good care of it. I'll wrap it in this piece of deerskin and my old quilt," Jamie said as he wrapped it carefully. "How about my putting it in this drawer?"

"Now you are all packed, and Mr. Allen and Mr. Busby are ready to place your things in the wagon."

Jamie felt sad to leave everything he knew, but once they were on their way, he was really excited to be a part of the wagon train.

Some of the leaves were big enough to make shadows on the dirt roadway where Jamie Bacon followed the covered wagon train. He echoed the call of the meadowlark. He watched the cattle ambling along in front of him. Herding them wasn't so bad. They just followed the train of canvas–topped wagons, and he walked behind them. He wondered why he had thought it would be a hard job. Jamie also wondered about his father, why he still had to be a soldier after the Revolutionary War was over. Being left alone by his mother's illness, then death, his family friends had agreed to take him along with them to the Northwest Territory. At least by going west he was more apt to find his father.

As Jamie listened to the wooden wagon wheels rolling on the hard, packed earth, the voices of drivers calling to their teams, the playful voices of children as they ran alongside the wagons, and the flap of canvas tops in the gentle spring air, he was sure he, and the cattle, could probably follow the train with their eyes closed.

Jamie would have liked to know how far they had already come since they left Front Royal, Virginia. Seeing a nice flat rock he picked it up and walked towards the Potomac River. He drew back his arm, and with the flick of his wrist, he sent the rock skipping across the water.

"Oh, that skipped way out there!" Jamie laughed as he turned to find another nice flat rock. To his horror, he saw that the wagon train was getting a long way ahead. He picked up the big stick he used for prodding the cattle, only to discover they had left the roadway and wandered into the nearby woods.

"Annabelle, Annabelle, you blasted animal! Here, get back on the road! No, don't go further away." The other cattle followed her. Yelling and running as fast as he could, Jamie stepped in the middle of a fresh *cowflop*. His foot slipped, and he fell so hard, it knocked the wind out of him. He finally could take a deep breath. He tried to stand, and a terrible pain exploded in his ankle. He fell back again. What was that terrible smell? Oh, he hadn't. He couldn't have, but he had.

No, this couldn't happen. He had promised Mr. Estes he would do a good job to earn his way. All of this because that Annabelle had run into the woods. Maybe it was because he had skipped a rock across the Potomac. He couldn't run. He was almost sick. The cattle were in the woods, and the wagon train was nearly out of sight. He would never find Pa. Teddy Hillis would laugh himself sick if he knew how Jamie had fallen.

Drying his tears, he picked up his big herding stick, and using it as a cane, he hobbled toward the roadway. Oh, it hurt his ankle so badly to walk! He waved his arms frantically and yelled as loud as he could at the disappearing wagon train. It just kept going.

Hot tears rolled from his eyes, for, suddenly, he felt forsaken and so all alone. But surely they wouldn't leave him, for they couldn't get along without their cattle.

Painfully, he tried to round up the cattle. He'd never be able to live this down with Jim and Teddy Hillis. Ever since their mother had given Jamie cookies they thought they should have had, they had never stopped teasing him. Teddy, especially, seemed to think he did so many funny things. Jamie looked down at his pants and nearly lost his breakfast, for his pants were covered with *cowflop*.

He continued to hobble, as best he could, to head off the cattle. This time he watched where he stepped. "Get back on the road, Annabelle. Don't just stand there chewing your cud and looking at me! If you only knew how I hurt!" He waved his big stick, yelled, then got around to where he could prod Annabelle. "Get back on the roadway, now! Go, you dumb beasts!"

He could not seem to push the cattle back to the road.

Mrs. Allen, in whose wagon he rode, was very kind to him. She had been his mother's best friend. She and her mother, Grandma Nelson, would help him get cleaned up if he ever saw them again.

"Why did my mother have to get sick and die? Where is Pa? What can I do?" Fresh tears rolled down his cheeks again. They just can't leave me back here all alone. They need their cattle.

In the distance, he heard, then saw, a couple of men on horseback coming toward him. It was the wagon master! He couldn't let Mr. Estes see him crying. He wiped his tears on his sleeves.

As the horses reigned to a stop, Mr. Estes called out, "Jamie, boy, what happened?"

Jamie knew if he tried to talk he would burst into tears. What could he do?

"Here I thought I could depend on you. Why aren't you rounding up the cattle? How did they get away from you?" demanded Mr. Estes.

How could Jamie answer? He was afraid Mr. Estes would put him off of the wagon train for losing the cattle. He didn't want him to know he had stepped into that stinking fresh *cowflop*. His blond head was down, and his blue eyes were brimming with tears. Mr. Estes must never know he had been skipping rocks across the river.

Jamie was sure Mr. Estes already saw and smelled the *cowflop* all over his boots and pants.

"I tried to round up the cattle, but my ankle hurts so badly, I couldn't.

"Son," said Mr. Estes, as he jumped off of his horse, stooped down, and grabbed two handfuls of grass. He held the grass between the boot and his hands to help Jamie get his boot off. "Try to move your foot around."

"It hurts so badly, but I'll try."

"I can tell it is badly sprained. Use your herding stick as a cane, and let's go down to the river. We can get you cleaned up a bit," Mr. Estes suggested.

At the river, Mr. Estes knelt next to Jamie and splashed handfuls of water onto his pants and boots.

While he helped him clean up, he said, "Jamie, you are big enough to handle a few cows. You have to keep your eyes on them all of the time so that when they start to wander off, you go right after them. You don't realize, young man, how bad any delay is for the wagon train. Careful plans have been made for further along. Don't ever let it happen again!"

Jamie was afraid to speak for he was so near to crying, but he did look up at Mr. Estes.

"Now, son, we'll put you on my horse. Bring your boot and sock. I see Mr. Pruitt has about rounded up all of the cattle."

Shortly before the two men had all of the cattle back on the roadway, Mr. Estes said to Jamie, "I was hoping I wouldn't step into what you did, Jamie."

Jamie didn't know whether he wanted to laugh or cry.

As Mr. Estes jumped back on his horse with Jamie he said, "Learn to keep your eyes and your mind on your job. Where would the wagon train be if I didn't keep my mind on my work? Here, I'll take your herding stick. When we reach Ohio, there may still be Indians who could give us trouble. Let's go. Keep your eyes on the cattle. I am sorry your ankle hurts so badly."

It was such a relief for Jamie to get to ride. "Will the Indians attack our train? I have my grandfather's gun, but I don't know how to use it," Jamie said shyly.

"You aren't big enough and strong enough to handle it yet, but I expect some day you will be able to use it very well. I know your grandfather was a soldier and fought under General George Washington."

"That's right, he had told me about it many times."

Jamie would have liked to have told him more, but his ankle hurt so badly he didn't want to say much. Almost in tears, Jamie did say, "I sure hope I can find Pa real soon."

"I know about your soldier pa, too. President Jefferson sent him someplace where he cannot be reached. We will all keep looking. We'll inquire for him at each army post, and someday we'll find him. Don't you worry."

Everyone was waiting for them as they rounded the bend and came in sight of the big, white-topped wagons. The horses were stomping their feet and making noises. They probably were telling the cattle they were glad to see them and to get a move on so they could get going again.

Jamie was glad to be back with the Allens. He desperately hoped no one knew what really happened.

For the rest of the day, Helen and Ruth were assigned to his job of cowherding. When Mr. Estes delivered Jamie to the Allen wagon he said, "Jamie needs to be cleaned up and must stay off of his sprained ankle for some time. I'll leave it up to him to tell you what happened."

Mrs. Allen and Grandma Nelson took him inside the wagon where he could strip off his pants. He crawled into his bed. His ankle had become painfully swollen, so he was glad to lay down. His bed was made of his chest of drawers laid flat. Inside the chest and on top were all of his belongings, including the oil painting of Washington on his horse. The Allens' bed was across the back of the wagon. Grandma Nelson's bed was nearer the Allens' and on one side. Jamie's bed was nearer the wagon seat on the other side.

Grandma Nelson's rocking chair had to be set on top of his bed during the day when they needed more floor space. Barrels, boxes, a trunk, and packages were stuffed or hung all around inside and outside of the wagon.

The smell of new paint, new wood, and leather inside the wagon was comforting to Jamie. Sunshine coming through the canvas top gave a soft yellowish light. Jamie listened to the sounds of people, horses, cattle, and dogs with the squeak of wheels as they rolled along the rutted and bumpy dirt road.

After Mrs. Allen helped him get cleaned up and put him to bed, she brought him some johnnycake. Grandma Nelson sat in her rocking chair and told him tales of long ago as they rode along.

"Grandma Nelson, do you think the Indians will attack our wagon train when we get out of Virginia?"

"Mercy, Jamie, where did you get such an idea? This is the year of eighteen and four. The Indian battles have been settled with treaties. They would be more likely to attack us while we go down the Ohio River. I believe our trip will be safe."

When they stopped for the night, Mr. Hillis came to their wagon and brought a crutch he had made for Jamie. He said, "I know that my boys like to tease you, but, that is just part of growing up. Try to hand it back sometime."

"Oh, thank you Mr. Hillis, for the crutch. Now I can help Mrs. Allen." To himself he thought, *Mr. Hillis, you just don't know how much I'd like to hand it back to Teddy and Jim*, but he simply couldn't do it.

That evening, after they had eaten and prepared for the night, the entire wagon train of folk had a meeting. Their wagon master, Mr. Estes, was highly respected. His aides, Mr. Reeves and Mr. Watson, were delegated to keep all sixteen wagons in line, both in their travel and in camp.

When all were assembled, Mr. Estes talked to them about their crossing of the Potomac River the next day. He said they would cross in the order of their already assigned places. He pointed out the necessity for everyone to listen to orders and fulfill their obligations. They would need a lot of teamwork from everyone, young and old.

Jamie squirmed where he sat, thinking Mr. Estes might tell of Jamie's negligence with the cattle as a bad example, but he kindly omitted it.

Mr. Estes continued by explaining how their timetable had to be kept, for when they arrived in Pittsburgh, other wagons, which would have come over the Allegheny Mountains, would be there also. So many people needing and wanting to get their keel boats built made a time schedule necessary.

"Of course, as you know, some folks will continue on by land, but our route takes us to Marietta, Ohio, by the Ohio River. I feel it is easier and safer that way. Sleep well, for tomorrow will be a busy day."

Jamie vowed to himself, *Whatever they ask me to do tomorrow, I am going to do it like a man.*

He would never find pa if they should leave him behind.

He used his crutch to walk back to the wagon. He felt sure Mr. Hillis had not known how he happened to sprain his ankle. He and Mr. Estes were really kind people. Mr. Hillis reminded him of his pa.

River Crossing

It was midmorning when the wagon train folks reached their chosen place for crossing the Potomac River. Jamie couldn't decide whether he was more anxious or more scared when he thought of going across.

Almost everyone ran to the river's edge to see how it looked. To his hand, the water felt cold.

Before long, we'll know how it feels, thought Jamie.

The wagons were already lined up in the order of crossing. After looking at the river, most hurried back to their wagons, except the children. They were pitching rocks and twigs into the water and asked Jamie to join them.

"Hey, Jamie, see if you can throw a rock out there as far as I can," teased Teddy.

The memory of his skipping a rock across the river, and its consequences, made Jamie unhappy. "I just want to watch how the water runs," he answered. "Look at how the sunshine sparkles and dances on the surface of the water." The river did look peaceful. Once again, he could hardly wait for the crossing.

Jamie went back to the wagon when he saw Mr. Estes arriving. He had come to speak to Mr. Allen and to check their preparations.

"I want to make sure that you stowed everything so that it can't move when the wagon gets tossed about in the river," Mr. Estes advised.

"I think you will find everything to your liking," said Mr. Allen.

"One more thing, I think you should tie that rocking chair to the wagon seat," said Mr. Estes.

"I am planning to sit in it," Grandma Nelson said.

"Now listen, you may think a little lady like yourself could keep the chair in place, but, I think it had better be tied, too."

"Well, Mr. Estes, I never think of myself as little, but tied it shall be. I guess the river current may be strong."

"Grandma Nelson, I can just see you bouncing along on the river in your rocking chair," Jamie said, while they all laughed at the imaginary picture.

"When that is done, will we be ready?" Mr. Allen asked.

"Yes, you folks have followed instructions well. I see you have everything else tied." With a big smile on his face he asked, "Jamie, would you be willing to help the Watson family?"

"Of course, what do they want me to do?"

"Their two little girls, Florence and Nellie, are to ride across on the back of one of their horses. I want you to make sure they don't slip off into the water," Mr. Estes said.

"But, sir, how can I? I don't know how to swim."

"Son, you won't need to swim. You are to hang on to the horse's tail and when the water gets deep, kick your feet hard. We used to do this when we were children, just for fun."

Seeing that Jamie hesitated, he added, "Maybe I should ask Teddy Hillis or one of the bigger boys."

He couldn't let Teddy get ahead of him on this one. "I'll do it," said Jamie, "I'll run over to the Watson wagon now."

As Mr. Estes turned to leave, he called back over his shoulder, "Mr. Allen, when it is your turn to enter the river, drive slowly and carefully. That old river probably has some boulders in it."

Jamie felt glad Mr. Estes trusted him enough to ask him to do something. He did not like Mr. Watson, for he had been cross with him and other children. In spite of his dislike for Mr. Watson, he was sure he could do this job right, like a grown-up. He just wished his heart would quit pounding so hard merely at the thought of it.

Grandma Nelson had told him one time that some children learn to swim by being thrown into the water. If only his pa were here, he wouldn't even feel scared.

When he found Mr. Watson, Mrs. Watson and the older girls were ready to go across inside the wagon. They looked scared but waved to Jamie and smiled.

"Do you know what it is you are to do?" asked Mr. Watson.

"Yes, Mr. Estes said I was to hang on to the horse's tail and call to you in case the two little girls start to slip off," said Jamie.

To himself, Jamie thought how easy it had sounded when Mr. Estes said it, but his stomach felt hollow. What if his hands slipped? What if the horse kicked him?

"Look how securely they are tied on to the horse's back," Mr. Watson said. "I'll be leading the horse. I am sure there will be a lot of motion when we get midstream. This is a very gentle horse. Make certain you keep hold of her tail."

Jamie tried to act unafraid as he assured Mr. Watson he would hang on and keep a watch on his little girls.

At last the big moment had come for the first wagon to enter the river. It was the Estes wagon. Two men on horseback, who led the horses that were pulling the wagon, also held ropes tied to the front of the wagon. Two other horsemen following the wagon carried ropes tied to the back of the wagon.

Mr. Estes drove his wagon so it rolled slowly into the river. Everybody seemed to be holding their breath. About midstream, the wagon made a quick turn as if it would go into a circle. With much shouting and straining of men and horses they pulled into the right direction. They slowly pulled up onto the other side.

Everyone clapped and yelled such things as, "They did it! Praise the Lord! Now we can all do it, too."

The same four horsemen came back and tied up to the Brackney wagon. It was the second wagon to cross. Following them would be the Watson wagon with Jamie holding on to the horse carrying the two little girls. Jamie wondered how his hands could be cold and sweaty at the same time. His teeth even chattered. He felt that everybody would be watching him go into the water, so he must not yell or complain. When the Brackney wagon started to turn over in midstream everyone screamed. Jamie watched horses and men strain every muscle and the men call commands to each other.

If the current does that to a big wagon, what will it do to me? worried Jamie.

They were able to get the wagon upright before it fell all the way over. Poor Mrs. Brackney and her daughters, Lucille and Helen, had managed to hang on to the wagon seat.

As they started up the other side of the river, Jamie knew it was Mr. Watson's and his turn next.

Jamie clung to the horse's tail as tightly as he could. His first step into the water took his breath. It was so cold. How could he keep going? He must. Every step he took was colder and deeper. When the water was up to his armpits, he jumped up and started kicking his feet furiously. He stayed on top of the water. *This is going to work*, Jamie thought. It did seem easy to stay afloat.

Suddenly, the horse jumped and began to thrash its legs wildly. The girls screamed. Jamie's hands began to slip along the tail. He clenched the tail. Still it slipped through his fingers.

"I can't hold on!" he bellowed.

The last bit of tail was gone. Water pulled at him, dragging him away from the horse. He opened his mouth to yell again, as he felt himself begin to sink. He snapped his mouth shut and held his breath. He flapped his arms wildly. The movement brought him out of the water. He sucked in air.

"Help!" he yelled.

The water pulled him under again.

I'll drown! If I could only breathe!

He felt his hair being pulled, then he was on someone's back. Gasping for breath, he clung to the man and could feel him walking through the water. Finally, he knew they were on land. The man laid him down on his stomach.

Jamie could feel the man pounding his back. "Cough up as much water as you can. I must get back on duty in case someone else needs me."

After coughing and coughing, Jamie was able to see better and get a good breath. Florence and Nellie sat nearby shaking and crying. He felt terrible that he'd even forgotten them. He remembered he was supposed to take care of them.

Jamie led the girls to where they could sit in front of a boulder, out of the wind and in the sunshine. The girls' mother came soon and wrapped them in a soggy quilt. She told them to stay right there until all of the wagons were across. They must stay out of the way.

Jamie was very nervous when they brought the Allen wagon across. The men were better prepared for the force of the river current in the deep section. Jamie was glad to see that no more wagons nearly went out of control. He could hardly wait to be with the Allens and Grandma Nelson.

When all of the wagons were across, they brought the cattle across. It took much prodding and yelling. They managed to get Annabelle started into the water, and the others followed.

Mrs. Watson came to get the girls. She thanked Jamie profusely.

"I hope you're all right. I heard that you went under the water a couple of times. No one expected that to happen," Mrs. Watson assured him.

"I'm sorry I wasn't of better help to the girls," Jamie answered.

"You have helped us very much. We are grateful to you, Jamie," Mrs. Watson answered. "Come girls," she said as she led the girls away. "Now you will have a wonderful story to tell to your grandchildren."

After all of the wagons, people, and animals were across, they went on higher ground and built a huge fire. There they exchanged their experiences and dried out their clothing.

It was a jubilant crowd who responded to Mr. Allen's, "Praise the Lord, we made it across. It's been a time to remember!"

Jamie was quiet and hoped he wouldn't be teased for nearly drowning, instead of being a help.

When Jamie found the Allens, Mrs. Allen gave him a big hug and said, "Jamie, dear, we watched your every move and prayed very hard when we saw you slip under the water."

Grandma Nelson threw her shawl around his shoulders, and kissing him on the forehead said, "Jamie, we are so thankful that you came through safely. We have already thanked Mr. Reeves, who pulled you out of the water. We must thank God we are all safe again."

"I wish that some time when Mr. Estes asked me to do something I could do it right," said Jamie. "Nearly drowning was a terrible experience. I never want to have it ever again."

Grandma Nelson said, "Jamie, for your own safety, you must learn to swim. Don't worry, there will be other chances for you to prove you can take responsibility. I heard the men talking about how the force of the current was far greater than they had expected. For now, let's get over to the fire and get warm.

Lost in a Crowd

After Jamie's wagon train had crossed the Potomac River, it took two weeks to reach Pittsburgh. They followed the Monongahela River after leaving the Potomac. We find them camped near Pittsburgh while their keelboats are being built.

It was Wednesday, market day in town. Mrs. Allen and her mother were anxious to buy some fresh produce.

"What can I take to the market to sell or trade?" Jamie asked.

"Would you want to part with that little bird you carved the other day?"

"Grandma Nelson, do you think anyone would want it?" asked Jamie.

"Of course, it looks so real. Jamie, you have a real talent for carving. Where is that bird's nest you found yesterday?"

Mrs. Allen told them it was still on the wagon seat. She added, "I believe it is just the right size, too."

"Thanks for such a good idea," Jamie said.

"And why don't you find two or three little stones that look like eggs to put into the nest," Grandma Nelson suggested, while handing him a piece of cloth. "Here, take this and tie your bird and nest in it so it will be easier to carry."

Mr. Estes had called them together soon after their arrival for instructions on how to go into the city. He cautioned them to always leave somebody with the wagon to guard their possessions. He suggested they go with and stay with someone when they went into the city. He warned that there would be many strangers. In that year of 1804, there were many folks who came across the Allegheny Mountains from the east into Pittsburgh.

Jamie could hardly wait to see the crowds of people. He would probably see hundreds of strangers.

Mrs. Allen, Grandma Nelson, and Jamie were going to town together. The women wore their Sunday dresses, long white aprons, and their bonnets. They each carried a basket.

"How would you like to put your carving in my basket?" Grandma Nelson asked.

"That would be nice, thanks," Jamie answered.

"Here, set it in this way. When we get into the market you can have it back," Grandma Nelson advised.

"I can hardly wait to see the big buildings," Jamie said as they walked along a well–trodden path.

"And I can hardly wait to see their market. I've heard it is huge, and they have a great variety of goods," Grandma Nelson added.

Before they came to the boatbuilders, Jamie had been running ahead. As he rounded a curve he could see buildings from which black smoke poured out of tall chimneys.

He stopped, stood still a few seconds, then called, "Stop, stand still a minute. Can you feel the ground shake?"

"Why, yes. Goodness me. That must come from the heavy pounding of iron and timbers being hammered at the shipbuilders," Grandma Nelson said.

"Mercy, I guess you are right," said Mrs. Allen. "Jamie, you will have to come with Mr. Allen another day to see how they work. For now, we must get along to where we get the ferry to cross the river."

They took the ferry, which was ready to cross when they arrived. They crossed the Monongahela River. They then climbed a steep hill. They saw more and more people the nearer they came to town.

Jamie said, "Did you hear how those people talked? I couldn't understand a word they said."

"I am pretty sure they are from Scotland. Yes, do you see the beautiful colors in their woolen, plaid clothing?" Grandma Nelson answered.

Before they reached the public square Jamie called, "Look at that tall brick building, it has a steeple." That one stood higher than those around it. "Do you think we can ever find the marketplace?"

"Careful, Jamie. In your excitement you almost bumped into Mother's basket. You could upset your bird and nest," said Mrs. Allen.

As they started to walk around the courthouse, they were surprised to bump into Mrs. Hillis and her children. Florence held a big piece of maple sugar candy, which she was obviously eating. "Oh, look. They have everything in the world in that market. This is the best candy I've ever tasted."

"Florence, you exaggerate a bit," said Mrs. Hillis, "but they do have wonderful garden produce, fine baked goods, and stalls where you can buy yard goods, needles, candles, and even frying pans. Oh, you will soon see for yourselves."

James and Teddy, Florence's brothers, each carried candy and a bow and arrows. "Come on, Jamie, let us show you where you can buy a bow and arrows like ours."

"Wait, I have to get my carving out of Grandma Nelson's basket. Is it all right for me to go with them?" Jamie asked as he took his carving out of the basket.

"Yes," replied Mrs. Allen. "Now, you boys stick together like Mr. Estes told us we should."

"We will," answered Jamie as the three boys started off together.

Mrs. Allen called after Jamie, "Good luck on selling your carving."

Through the big crowd Jamie could see the marketplace. Market stalls were lined up in a fan shape. In front of the stalls were hitching posts where horses, with buggies and wagons, were tied.

Jamie saw how the horses stood on straw, and a trough of water was nearby. Boys about his age seemed to be caring for the horses.

Jamie knew he could buy nothing until he sold his carving. He went with Teddy and James to see the hunting supply booth. They stopped at the next one where they sold carvings of ducks, birds, and animals.

Jamie finally edged up right next to the counter. "Please, sir," Jamie said. No clerk seemed to see or hear him. In spite of arms reaching over him, and being shoved, he asked, "Please sir, would you look at my bird?"

One clerk smiled at him, and taking his carving went to the other clerk. When he returned he asked, "Young man, would you be willing to let us have this whole thing, as it is, for one dollar?"

"Oh, yes sir," Jamie said. He had never expected to get so much for it. He timidly asked, "May I have the cloth back?"

As the clerk handed him the dollar and the cloth he said, "Did you carve the bird yourself?"

"Yes, I did, but the nest had fallen from a tree."

"This is very lifelike, son. Could you possibly bring us some more of your work?"

"I don't know, for we will be here just long enough to have our boat built."

"Let us know if you get any more carvings ready to sell," the clerk said.

Jamie nodded. When he turned to find James and Teddy, he soon discovered they were nowhere to be found.

I don't know anybody or which way to go to find our wagon train. He felt as if his insides had dropped out, he was so frightened.

"Oh, what shall I do? Pa, please help me." No use crying.

Suddenly, someone grabbed his arm and snatched the dollar out of his hand. He turned around and saw two dirty women. The one holding his arm wore a long blue skirt and ragged brown shawl. She would not let go of his arm.

"Let go of me!" he shouted. The other woman, in a long gray dress, grabbed his other arm. She put a filthy hand over his mouth very hard. He couldn't scream or even bite.

"Hush up, boy!" We'll buy you some bread and take you to a nice home to live in!"

"No!" he tried to holler. He kicked them, but the crowd was so thick his protests were unnoticed.

In a run, the women pulled Jamie until they entered a dark alley. Barking dogs and grunting pigs ran ahead of them.

I'll get away from you filthy women somehow, Jamie thought. He struggled and kicked them both, but could not get free.

A big man, who wore a shiny badge on a dark suit and carried a club, ran into the alley. "What are you two wretches doing with that boy?"

"He wants us to find him a home. We know where they is lookin' fer a servant boy."

Jamie squirmed and tried to yell. He thought the man was a lawman and could help him.

The lawman shoved the women back away from Jamie.

"Who are you, young man?"

"I am James Bacon from Virginia. My pa is a soldier."

"Is your pa here with you?"

Wiping his face and trying to ease the hurt of his mouth from being so tightly covered, Jamie answered. "No, I am with friends on a wagon train. We hope to find my pa somewhere out west."

The two women started to run away.

"Come back here and listen to me. Stealing a boy to sell as a servant is against the law. Do you understand?"

They meekly nodded and grunted.

"The next time I catch you two breaking the law, you will be put in the stocks and duly punished."

The women slipped away.

"Young man, let's get out of this stinking alley. You should have stayed with the folks who brought you into town."

"While I was selling my carving, the two boys I was with ran off and left me. When I saw they were gone, I didn't know which way to go to get back to the wagon camp."

"Were you scared?" asked the lawman.

"Yes, I felt sick to my stomach I was so scared. That wasn't as bad as when those crazy women grabbed me and stole my money."

"Well, I am sorry you lost your money, too. Look over there where I'm pointing. You can see the stocks where we put people who break the law."

"Yes, I see that. We have the same thing in Virginia."

"James, I have a son about your age. I'm not letting you out of my sight until I get you back to the wagon train. Come along now. Did you cross the river to get here?"

"Yes, sir, we did. My folks will be mighty glad if you'll get me home."

Together they started walking along by some shops. The lawman said, "My name is McDougall, and I already know your name."

"They don't call me James, but Jamie."

"And one day, it may be Jim," said Mr. McDougall.

"Oh, Mr. McDougall, what are they making in there?" asked Jamie as he pointed to the copper shop.

"They handle copper, which is used in many ways. They make large containers and many small kinds of hardware."

They passed a saddler shop, a wheelwright shop, a tobacconist, and tanners. "Oh, sir, would this be where they make things of leather?" Jamie asked.

"Yes, it's a leather tannery, and they also make things. Some of their products are displayed in their shop windows. Of course, you know they even make clothing from their leather."

A little further on Jamie caught Mr. McDougall's arm. "Please, Mr. McDougall, look, could we go in and watch them?"

"No, son, this is a printer's shop, and they are very busy. The strong smell is their ink."

It was a place Jamie would like to come back to see again, as well as the bakery that smelled so good as they passed.

"What do they print?" asked Jamie.

"They print anything anyone wants to have printed. They print calendars, books, pamphlets, and so on. They have a pamphlet on things one should know for going down the Ohio River. You folks should buy one."

"Maybe I can come back someday, but I am not sure I want to unless I can be with my pa."

"Just make certain you are with someone who will not leave you behind."

They passed a tobacconist and many other interesting shops.

"I must get you home and get back to town," Mr. McDougall said.

When Mr. McDougall and Jamie stepped off the ferry, Mr. Estes met them. "Jamie, I am so glad and relieved to see you."

"Thank you, Mr. Estes." He wanted to hug him, but instead he introduced Mr. McDougall to him. Only minutes before, Jamie had been thinking he would be so happy to see anybody he knew, their dogs, even Annabelle, the cow.

Mr. Estes shook hands with Mr. McDougall. He said, "We were all so worried about Jamie when we discovered that the Hillis boys came back without him. It was a joke to them."

Mr. McDougall said that there were so very many people converging on Pittsburgh. Some were undesirable and came only to steal from unsuspecting travelers. "They keep us busy," he said.

"On your way back, maybe you could come and see the forty-by-twelve-foot boat we are having built."

"Thank you, but when I get this fine lad home, I must get back into town. You know, duty calls."

"Perhaps you can return when the boat is nearly finished. It will have a shelter for the family as well as room on deck for our farm animals," said Mr. Estes.

"As I understand it, you folks then uses this lumber in building your cabins and barns."

"Yes, that is our plan," answered Mr. Estes.

"Well, good luck to you in all of your endeavors, Mr. Estes. I'll try to get back. Good day. Let's get on to camp, Jamie."

Mrs. Allen saw them coming and ran to meet them. "Lord of mercy, Jamie, we searched and searched for you. Sir, I can't tell you how thankful I am to you for bringing him back. Can you stay for a bite to eat?"

"No, as much as I'd like, I must go. Jamie had a close call. You might never have seen him again. Jamie, with all of the hugs you're getting, I know you must be glad to be back. I'll leave it up to you to tell them what happened."

Mr. McDougall shook hands all around as Mr. Hillis arrived.

"You must have brought our lad back to us. How grateful we are to you." Holding Jamie's carving up he said, "I just couldn't see some stranger having this, so I bought it. Maybe, you could make a carving for this lawman, Jamie," said Mr. Hillis.

"I certainly would like that," Jamie agreed.

"I am Mr. Hillis, and will see that you receive the carving," Mr. Hillis told the lawman. "You must have come down one street while I was on another. I was on Market and Hay Streets."

"Probably so." With a warm handshake for Jamie, he tipped his hat and left.

Jamie told his story of what had happened, including losing his dollar. He sat close to Grandma Nelson, who sat in her rocking chair. It was so good to feel safe again.

Campus Martius

Jamie had finished and sent the carving of a dog to Mr. McDougall in Pittsburgh. Nothing was more exciting than the news that their flatboat was ready to go on the Ohio River.

Jamie worked with the Reeves, the Allens, and the Allens' hired man, Mr. Busby, helping to load the flatboat. Their horses, cattle, and chicken crates fit on the deck in front of the shelter house, which was built in the middle of the deck.

In back of the shelter, they tied the wagons and all of the goods which were not needed on the boat. Even though a bit of wall was built around the sides of the boat to help contain everything, each animal and wagon was tied to the deck or shelter house.

"Should I feed and water the cattle and horses the same as usual?" asked Jamie. "Will they get hungry riding on the boat?"

"I really don't know. It is possible they may get even hungrier," answered Mr. Allen. "We'll give them as smooth a ride as possible. You know, we've a lot of sandbars, river debris, and possible storms."

What fun it was to ride on the river. Their boat was forty feet by twelve feet.

Jamie watched the men use the broadhorns from where they stood on the shelter house.

"Mr. Allen, would you let me stand up there and work a broadhorn?" Jamie asked.

"No, Jamie, you have no idea how much strength it takes to control these broadhorns. (Broadhorns was the name given to the long handle and broad paddle oars.) It takes a lot of muscle to get us around some of these curves in the river."

Glancing back at the river, Jamie saw a huge log coming fast toward them. "Quick. Look! A big log is headed right toward us from the river bank!" Jamie hollered.

Grandma Nelson shouted for Jamie to hold on to the shelter house. The two men managed to steer away from the log while Mr. Busby was ready to shove it back from hitting them. They all knew they could be another river casualty if the log hit. Other possible accidents were avoided in the same way. They made good use of their river map, which they had bought in the print shop in Pittsburgh.

After rounding a big curve in the river on the 4th of June 1804, Mr. Allen called to his wife, "Look ahead to your right, and you will see Marietta, Ohio." They had left Pittsburgh a little more than a week before.

Jamie could hardly wait to get there. He just knew his pa would be at the dock to meet them. There surely wasn't much further west where his pa could go. President Jefferson had said Pa was somewhere out west. They had come such a long distance already.

He searched the faces in the crowd waiting for them. Everyone from the Virginia wagon train who had come ahead of them was there. But, Jamie couldn't find his father. Oh, how his chest hurt from the disappointment of not seeing him.

"Hello, Jamie," greeted Mr. Estes. "Are you glad to be arriving in Ohio?"

"Uh, yes sir. Have you seen my pa yet?" Jamie asked.

"No, Jamie, but someday we will find him."

Jamie's disappointment made him want to hide someplace and cry. Instead, Mr. Allen put him to work. He helped carry their belongings ashore. Their boat had to be totally emptied for it would next be taken apart. The lumber would later be stacked at their new building site. Until they found their new land, they would camp here at Campus Martius.

Seeing the disappointment on Jamie's face, Mr. Allen said to him, "Jamie, they may know something about your pa here at the fort."

While carrying bedding from the shelter house on the boat, Jamie heard Mr. Estes telling them they had everything they needed in Campus Martius. They even had a church and a school. Also, he reported that the farm land looked fertile.

Mrs. Hillis, who had been at the dock to meet them, said they had not had any trouble with the Indians; however, they had been warned that some people had been robbed by hoodlum camp followers.

"We have nothing of value to anyone but us. We've brought no treasures," said Mrs. Allen.

"How about Jamie's oil painting?" asked Grandma Nelson. "It would probably bring a pretty penny if sold."

"Yes, I expect it would," agreed Mrs. Allen. "We'll have to make sure someone is always at our wagon."

Had Grandma Nelson and Mrs. Allen known two hoodlums were in the crowd, they would not have mentioned the oil painting.

It was dark before they were settled in their camp. They all went to bed early, really glad to be through with the river travel.

The next morning, as soon as the chores and breakfast were finished, Jamie was on his way to see the walled fort called Campus Martius. A summer shower made every step he took a wet one. The sun had just come out. It felt warm on his head and shoulders. He loved the smell of the wet earth.

"What is that?" He almost stepped on the biggest fishing worm he had ever seen in his whole life. Picking it up, he wondered if the Allens would let him have a fishhook so he could go fishing. "There will surely be others. I'm anxious to find out if anyone has seen Pa. Good bye, fat worm."

He gave it a whirl so that it circled before it hit the ground.

Families who had come to Ohio before this year already had gardens. It was market day. Jamie searched every face at the market but did not see his pa. He saw a wonderful display of baked goods.

"Mmm, if he only had something to trade." Another booth had carrots, onions, beets, and cabbage. At one booth, they even had apples. Jamie noticed that people often exchanged things instead of using money.

Maybe Jamie could trade his last carving, a pig, for some apples. They had meats, but he didn't know what kind of meats they were.

Jamie saw Mr. Harrison talking to a man who was dressed in a white shirt but had no hat. He joined them. He noticed the stranger had three pencils in his shirt pocket and wore a canvas apron. He was telling Mr. Harrison that the soil around there was very good for farming.

"This is Jamie, Mr. Greenwood," said Mr. Harrison. "He is one of our folk from Virginia. And now, I'd best be getting back to my family."

"Good morning, young man," greeted Mr. Greenwood. "I run the store here in Campus Martius. What can I do for you?"

"I am looking for my pa and thought maybe he'd be here in Marietta," said Jamie.

"What makes you think he would be here?"

"When my mother was so ill, Mr. Allen went to Washington, D.C. President Jefferson said Pa was somewhere in the west. He would send word of his wife's illness, but had no idea when he would receive it. He was sorry. His pa was on a secret mission."

"Then what happened?" Mr. Greenwood asked.

"My mother died." Tears still came in Jamie's eyes when he talked about his mother.

Mr. Greenwood patted Jamie's shoulder and pressed a handkerchief into his hand.

"Mrs. Allen was my mother's best friend and wanted me to come west in their wagon."

"I am sorry things have gone so badly for you. Tell me, what is your last name?" asked Mr. Greenwood.

"My name is James Bacon. My grandfather Bacon was a soldier, too. He fought under General George Washington.

"Well, son, there will be a lot of people here today. Keep your eyes open for Mr. John Chapman. He carries a double pouch and has a really big beard. You will recognize him."

"And you think he may know something about Pa?" asked Jamie.

"Yes. He plants apple seeds where he goes, and preaches. He is well known by a lot of people, and he remembers them. He came here from Pennsylvania. He may have seen your father some time."

"I'll sure watch for him. Here comes Grandma Nelson. We are hoping to get some fresh vegetables today."

"I thought you had no family," Mr. Greenwood said.

"She is Mrs. Allen's mother and treats me as if I were her grandson. She is lots of fun and can do anything."

"Greetings, Mrs. Nelson. Your fine lad, Jamie, has already told me your name."

"How good to get to meet you! I'll wager that you are the storekeeper, aren't you?"

"Yes. You guessed it right. I was just telling Jamie about some people he might meet here who may have seen his pa."

A burst of happy sounds came from across Campus Martius. Glancing in that direction, Mr. Greenwood said, "What is going on? It is the Long Hunter. Come along, Jamie. It was good to meet you, Mrs. Nelson."

As Jamie and the grocer neared the cluster of people, a man with a heavy beard called out to Mr. Greenwood.

"Hey there, Mr. Greenwood, how about letting me leave my cargo in your store for a few days?"

"Sure, you are welcome to leave it there." Looking at Jamie, "Son, how about helping the Long Hunter unload furs from his boat?" asked Mr. Greenwood.

Jamie felt a rush of excitement. He'd never seen anyone dressed in worn and torn leather clothes before. In spite of a big grizzly beard, he saw very blue, sparkling eyes in a happy face. "Sure, I'll be glad to help."

As they worked to unload the boat, Jamie asked, "Why do folks call you the Long Hunter?"

"I stay out hunting a long time. One of these days, though, I'm going to settle down. I'm a singing teacher. I'll soon have a singing school session right here in Marietta."

"Young man, who was that fine looking lady with you?" asked the Long Hunter. "Will she be joining in the square dancing later?"

"She is Grandma Nelson. Yes, she loves to square dance. She is supposed to teach me how to dance one of these days."

"Will you tell her I want a dance with her this afternoon?"

"Sure will," answered Jamie.

Hesitating, but anxious, Jamie asked, "I wonder if you ever met a soldier with the name of John Bacon?"

"Well, let me think a minute. I often have soldier travelers spend a night in camp with me." Jamie noticed how big some of the torn places were in the Long Hunter's leather jacket. He wore heavy boots and a wide–brimmed hat. Deep lines ran from the corners of his eyes. "Yes, yes, I remember him well. A handsome man. He told me a very interesting story."

"Please tell me, had he killed a bear?" Jamie asked.

"Oh, no, nothing like that. His story was about his beautiful wife and how he practically carried away his bride from another man who hoped to marry her."

"Well then, that was not my pa," Jamie said. "I'm sure my mother never was about to marry anyone but Pa."

Jamie found the bundles hard to hang onto and very heavy, but soon the boat was empty and the goods safely stacked in the store.

"Son, you have been such good help I wonder if you would like to go further down on the Ohio River with me someday?"

"Oh, really, could I?"

"We shall have to talk more about it later. Don't forget to tell your grandmother I want a dance with her this afternoon."

Jamie took his leave and soon found Grandma Nelson. When he told her the Long Hunter's story of the soldier taking his bride from another man, she looked deeply into Jamie's eyes. She'd never looked at him that way before.

Finally, looking up and pointing she said, "Look at that man."

"Who could he be?" Grandma Nelson asked. "He is as weather–beaten at your Long Hunter friend. Look at that huge pouch."

"That is probably a double pouch, and his beard, come along. That is just the way Mr. Greenwood said the man from Pennsylvania would look. Let's go speak to him."

Others had gathered around him. Nearing the crowd Jamie heard one of the pretty girls say, "Sir, can you guess what name we have given you?"

"No, what could it be?" answered John Chapman.

"From now on, instead of John Chapman, we are going to call you Johnny Appleseed."

"Well, I certainly won't object to that one. Look here," he said, taking a handful of apple seeds from one side of the pouch. "I've plenty to plant. Someday a weary traveler will be thankful to feed his body with a refreshing apple. You see, in the other side I have food for the soul." He showed them his much worn Bible.

"In spite of our very cold winter, your trees are growing well," said a bystander.

"We are very thankful to you for making way for the stranger," called another bystander.

"That way I am serving our Lord," Johnny Appleseed said.

Jamie decided he would try to speak to him later. In the distance he could hear violins tuning up. "Grandma Nelson, you promised to teach me the Virginia Reel. Don't forget. Oh, I almost forgot, I am supposed to tell you that the Long Hunter wants to dance with you."

"That sounds like a good idea. Let's hurry and take these vegetables and bread back to the wagon then return to dance."

Before they started back from the wagon, Grandma Nelson took off her apron and wore a fresh white collar.

When they returned to the dance, they found the first reel dancing. "Now, when they form another group, you and I are going to join it right away," Grandma Nelson said.

The music made Jamie want to dance. Before long, they were lined up ready to dance. But, to his horror, he saw Florence Hillis was in the same group.

I wish I could get away from here, he thought. "Grandma Nelson, I don't want to dance this time." To himself he thought, *I'll probably stumble and bump right into silly Florence.*

"Now, Jamie," answered Grandma Nelson, "I am not letting my partner leave me. Don't be so shy. It will be fun, you will see."

All went well until the promenade. Instead of taking her hand as he should have, he held his hand a few inches away from Florence's. She reached and grabbed his hand and squeezed it hard. As soon as he could, he got free of her and left right after the reel was finished.

While Grandma Nelson danced the next reel, and many more, with the Long Hunter, Jamie went and sat close to the fiddlers. The vibrations of fiddle music made his chest tingle.

Look how they can get so many tunes from just four strings, Jamie thought. When the fiddlers stopped for a while, one of them asked, "Young man, did you ever try to play a fiddle?"

"Oh, no, I have never been this close to one before. Could you let me hold yours for a minute?"

"Of course, but you must be very careful how you handle it, you see, it is made of very thin wood. I brought it all the way from New York. I brought extra strings, for they break easily."

Gently taking the fiddle, Jamie carefully ran his hand along its body. "It feels so smooth, almost like the silk in a milkweed pod. What is the white dust under the strings?" Jamie asked.

"That is from the resin used on the bow. It helps the bow get a better sound from the strings. We are about ready to start again."

As he took the fiddle from Jamie, the fiddler said, "I know of a man who has a fiddle for sale. Would you like it?"

"Yes, yes, but I have to ask the Allens about it. Thank you, but right now we don't even have our cabin built. I want a dog, too."

"Well, in good time, you may have both."

Jamie listened to the music for a while then walked away wondering how there could be so many exciting things to learn about and he bumped into Teddy Hillis.

"Well, Jamie, did you find a girl for dancing?"

Jamie knew Florence had given Teddy the details, so he didn't answer. He walked on. Someday he would go west with the Long Hunter and forget Teddy and his sister.

Catching sight of Mrs. Allen with her purchases, Jamie ran to help her. She gave him her smaller basket to carry. He could hardly wait to see what she had bought.

"Mrs. Allen, I helped the Long Hunter carry some of his furs from his boat to the store. I saw Johnny Appleseed, I danced a reel with Grandma Nelson, and I got to hold a fiddle."

"It has been an exciting day for you. And do you know that very soon we will be settled on our own land? I can hardly wait. In the meantime we'll stay right here."

"I can hardly wait either. Maybe Pa will come to Marietta one day and want to live here, too."

Mrs. Allen had bought some fresh green onions that smelled so good. Jamie felt as if his feet hardly touched the ground as they carried their packages to the wagon. *I hope President Jefferson sent a message to Pa about our going to Ohio. If I think really hard about how much I want Pa to live here, maybe he will somehow receive my thoughts.*

In a Cave

The Allens, the Reeves, and several other Virginia wagon train folks remained camped at Marietta while acquiring their land location in the Northwest Territory.

Their children had lost some school days while traveling, so Mrs. Hillis, a former teacher, held school sessions on the grass by the Hillis wagon.

Jamie didn't mind going to school, but he had just found a piece of wood he wanted to carve. He could see a dove sitting on a rail fence in the grain of the wood. He'd have to wait until after school to start it.

When Jamie returned to his wagon, he found Mrs. Allen, Mrs. Reeves and her baby, and Grandma Nelson sitting on their beds making rag rugs. He overheard Grandma Nelson say, "Yes, he is not only a good dancer, but we both grew up in Baltimore."

"Does this mean, Mother, that we have a budding romance amongst us?" Mrs. Allen asked.

"Well, maybe, but you know there would be little satisfaction being settled down with a Long Hunter. When would you see him?"

They all laughed.

"I see Jamie is back," said Mrs. Allen, "Looks like he's found another hunk of wood for carving."

Jamie placed his carving wood in back of a front wagon wheel. He decided to take his oil painting to school.

"Grandma Nelson, may I lay some of my things on your bed?" Jamie asked. He climbed into the wagon.

"Of course, Jamie, but whatever are you doing?" asked Grandma Nelson.

"Be sure you put everything back or we might use it in our rug making," said Mrs. Allen. "Oh Jamie, don't look so frightened. I was only teasing you."

I decided to take my George Washington oil painting to school so my schoolmates can see it," Jamie said as he started to pull things out of the drawers. His chest of drawers, lying flat, served as his bed. In, or on it, were all of his belongings. "Oh, here it is still wrapped in my old quilt. I've missed seeing it," he said as he removed the quilt.

"Turn it this way so I can see it," said Mrs. Allen. "Your mother loved and cared for that picture very much."

"Looking at the picture makes me feel as if Mother is here with me," Jamie said.

"You know, Jamie, if that picture could talk, we might hear some amazing stories. Think of the danger it was in when the artist painted it somewhere near the battlefield of Fort Duquesne in 1755. Oh my, see how young George Washington was when that was painted," Grandma Nelson said.

"Yes, that is when my grandfather fought with Washington," said Jamie proudly.

"And think of the near disasters we had on our trip out here. Do you remember when a big log almost slammed into our flatboat?" asked Grandma Nelson.

"Yes, think what would have happened to us all," said Mrs. Reeves. "Even if we could have swum to shore, all of our belongings would have been lost."

"I can never forget that, or when an oncoming boat almost ran into us," recalled Mrs. Allen.

Jamie was listening as he repacked his chest of drawers. "I heard them say that Mr. William Henry Harrison is here helping to make the land settlements."

"I wonder if we settlers have to be afraid of the Indians?" asked Mrs. Reeves.

"From all that I've heard, we shouldn't be afraid of them, but I would just as soon others do the dealing," Grandma Nelson answered.

"Mrs. Pruitt's husband told her that the Northwest Territory covers more land than we have seen since leaving Pittsburgh," Mrs. Allen said. "Well, I see you are ready to go, Jamie. Thanks for putting your things away."

Whistling the dance tune, "Pop Goes the Weasel," Jamie trotted through the woods carrying his oil painting securely under his arm. When he was half way there, he suddenly stopped whistling for he felt someone was following him.

He looked back but saw only a squirrel's beady eyes watching him.

When he arrived at the Hillis wagon, the school children were lustily singing all of the verses of "Yankee Doodle." They made up several more verses. Jamie joined in as he sat down.

First, they had arithmetic. Why was it that Teddy Hillis could always answer the arithmetic problems first? He even did it while he pulled Rachel's braid when she sat next to Jamie, so she would think he had done it.

Their second lesson was spelling. They learned not only how to spell the words, but they had to know their meaning and use each word in a sentence.

"Does anyone have a recitation for us today?" Mrs. Hillis asked.

Rachel wildly waved her hand, and Mrs. Hillis gave her permission to speak. "I don't have a recitation, but I have a good riddle. May I please tell it?"

"My dear child, yes you may. Go ahead," said Mrs. Hillis.

"What is older than Adam if Adam were alive, just four weeks old and shall never be five?"

Their guesses of a mushroom and egg yolk were wrong. Even Teddy could not think of an answer.

Rachel shook her head. "If everybody gives up, I'll tell you. It is the moon."

Andrew asked, "Could Sarah please recite 'The Taking Girl'?"

Mrs. Hillis answered that she had done it so recently, she would like someone to recite a piece they hadn't heard before. "Let me know when any of you has a recitation memorized."

Shyly, Jamie raised his hand for permission to speak.

"I do know another riddle, but I want to show you my oil painting."

"Good, I was hoping that was what you brought with you."

Jamie could feel every eye on him as he unrolled the quilt, then the doeskin wrapper. He held the painting so all could see it.

"After my grandfather fought under General George Washington at Fort Duquesne, he was on his way home, almost back to Front Royal, when he came upon a British soldier. The soldier begged to exchange an oil painting for my grandfather's horse."

"Did he let him have his horse for that old picture?" asked Teddy.

"Yes," answered Jamie. "The English soldier needed to get back to Norfolk to catch his ship for England. My grandfather felt sorry for him. The picture is worth a lot of money. Since George Washington became president of our country, my mother said its value had become greater. She had it framed for she thought George Washington was a very fine person, and we all loved the picture. The artist is unknown. Mother made me promise to always take good care of it."

"How did it happen that an Englishman had a picture of an American general?" asked Andrew.

"The English soldier told my grandfather that he had taken it in payment for a debt."

"I wonder why those two dirty men were watching us from behind some trees," Sarah called out while pointing toward the woods.

Mrs. Hillis said, "Never mind, they are probably just hunters. Jamie, you had better take the painting back to your wagon and return for our reading class."

"I'll be right back," Jamie called as he left.

Jamie started toward their wagon tightly holding the rewrapped oil painting.

He had a strong feeling someone was watching him. He began to run as fast as he could. "Help!" He heard steps coming fast behind him! They got faster! He tried to run even faster. He screamed, "Help me, help me!" Is it a wild animal, an Indian? A terrible pain filled Jamie's shoulders and neck as claw–like hands grabbed his shoulders.

"Stop, you are hurting me! Let go-o." A big hand clamped over Jamie's mouth. Jamie could no longer yell as he fought the iron grip they had on him.

"Shut up, you towheaded brat! This will fix you so you'll stop that hollerin'." His captors were filthy men with their caps pulled down over their dirty faces. The one with only two big yellow teeth forced the painting from him while the other tied a rag around his mouth.

Both of the men picked him up by his pants and suspenders. They ran very fast. After a ways, they dropped him, took hold of his hands, and ordered him to run. He was so out of breath when he saw the entrance of a cave. He tried to shout, "No, no, no, don't make me go in there!" He dragged his feet to stop them.

Into the dark, damp, scary cave they went. Jamie could not stop them by squirming and kicking. They set him down on a boulder. The painting was dropped carelessly. Jamie tried to shout to take care of his mother's painting. His tears and effort to yell made them laugh.

They made sure the rag around his mouth was tight, and they used plenty of rope to tie him to the boulder.

"Stop that bellowin' or we'll whale the stuffin' outa ya. There is no use carryin' on fer you'll never be found and will rot here."

"We is gonna sell yer picture and git rich." With that, they left him.

When they had gone, Jamie yelled and yelled until he was hoarse. The only answering sound was the echo in the cave. He dropped his head. How long had he been there? He started twisting his head. After many tears, straining, and rope burns he did get the rag down off of his face.

Being able to breathe better he also heard better. Some place, water was dripping far away. How would he ever get out of there? How would he ever find his pa? With those thoughts, he again cried until he was exhausted.

Rescue

Jamie felt so lonely, tired, and afraid. He'd tried so hard, but he could not get loose from the ropes which tied him to the boulder. How could he ever get out and find his pa? Hope was gone. Tears had not helped.

Suddenly there was less light in the dreary cave. Something must be coming through the entrance. Jamie listened and was sure he heard slow footsteps coming closer. Would those horrible hoodlums be coming back? Could it be a wild animal?

He saw a man coming into the cave. He sat so still, he tried not to even blink his eyes. In the dim light, it took a while to see that the man was an Indian!

The Indian walked over to Jamie. Though it was cool in the cave, Jamie knew his clothes were wet with the sweat of fear. The Indian and Jamie looked at each other for a long time. Surely, the Indian heard his heart pounding. *What will happen next?* Jamie thought. He had never been this close to an Indian before.

At last, the Indian smiled in a friendly way. Jamie let out a big breath. The dreadful fear and loneliness were taken over by hope that he might escape the cave.

The Indian pointed to the rope holding Jamie. He pointed to himself, rolled his hands, then spread them apart.

"Yes, yes, untie me quick," said Jamie.

While untying Jamie, the Indian spoke a language Jamie could not understand. He spoke in a gentle voice. The instant Jamie felt free of the ropes, he wanted to run out of the cave as fast as he could. The Indian pressed his shoulder and shook his head. Jamie understood and realized that the hoodlums might want to capture him again.

When the Indian was ready, Jamie followed the Indian out of the cave.

When outside, Jamie wanted to shout for joy. He looked up at the blue sky and thought he had never seen such a beautiful day before. The air felt warm and smelled clean. He noticed that the trees had many colors he had never before noticed.

They hurried quietly through the woods. After some time passed, Jamie thought he heard his name called in the distance. He stopped the Indian, who had heard the call but didn't know it was for him. Jamie pointed to himself and said, "Jamie."

They heard the call again closer that time.

As loud as he could, he answered, "Here I am with a friendly Indian." He and the Indian stood still just off of a clearing. Soon they saw Mr. Allen ride into the clearing. Jamie went running toward him, and the Indian followed. "Here I am, Mr. Allen. This good Indian found me tied up in a terrible cave."

Mr. Allen jumped off of his horse, gave Jamie a big hug, and had a long handshake with the Indian. He started explaining how he should alert the rest of the posse that he had found Jamie. He saw that the Indian didn't understand so he pointed to Jamie, pointed to the surrounding woods, and then placed two fingers on the gun. He raised the gun toward the sky and shot twice. The posse would know he had been found.

"Jamie, do you have any idea if the painting is somewhere around?" Mr. Allen asked.

"No, I don't know where they went after they tied me in the cave," Jamie answered. "Oh, here comes Mr. Estes and Mr. Pruitt."

"Jamie," they called. "You are safe. Thank the Lord." They joined up with Jamie, the Indian, and Mr. Allen. Jamie could hardly wait to tell them what happened.

"I was tied up in a cave, and this kind Indian found me and untied me." The two men dismounted and shook hands with the Indian and Jamie. Although the Indian couldn't understand their words, he must have understood their meaning of how grateful they were to him.

The Indian pointed to his ear, then to Jamie's cheeks and motioned tears falling. He pointed to himself and gestured going into the cave, so they all understood that he had heard Jamie crying. Before he left, Mr. Allen gave him his pocketknife. The Indian seemed very appreciative, bowed, and disappeared.

"Yes, now we can get you back home, Jamie," said Mr. Allen. "Up on my horse you go."

Some of Jamie's friends heard then saw Mr. Allen bringing him home through the woods. They ran to meet them.

"Oh Jamie, what happened to you? I heard you shouting for help, and it really scared me," said Sarah.

"Did those ugly men we saw in the woods get you? Did they get the picture?" asked Andrew.

It seemed to Jamie they were all talking at once. He was happy to know so many were thankful he was back. His relief at being out of such an awful cave could be matched by nothing he had ever known.

People came to greet his return. They all were interested to know an Indian had helped him, especially after he told them what the hoodlums had done to him.

When they all had eaten, the men planned another posse to search for the hoodlums. Men from the fort wanted to join. Several local people had had things stolen.

Jamie wanted nothing so much as to be with Grandma Nelson in the wagon. He curled up on his bed and went to sleep while she sat by him.

When he awoke, the first thought he had was of the terrible cave and those two mean men. Grandma Nelson reminded him of the carving he wanted to start. His hands didn't feel like carving, but he did get the wood and started to work on it. Time always did fly fast when he was working on a carving. He knew that with as hard as he had to think about the carving, he might almost forget the cave a little.

When it was almost dark, Mr. Reeves arrived back at the wagon camp. Everyone gathered to hear his report. He said Mr. Allen had stayed with the men who were marching the two, tied-together hoodlums into the fort. There, the law would handle them.

"How did you catch them?" asked Jamie.

"Actually, it was your little quilt we saw first. They had placed the wrapped painting into the crotch of a tree. They were asleep nearby on the ground."

"They probably do most of their work at night," said Grandma Nelson. "How did you go about catching them?"

"We awakened them with a gun in each of their faces. They knew they were caught. They even tried to run. They claimed that the picture was theirs. They planned to sell it and get rich enough to buy land in Cairo," Mr. Reeves told them.

"Mr. Allen has the painting now. Jamie, we are so grateful to the Indian, for when he heard you cry, he rescued you."

"It is good to know there are friendly and good Indians around here," said Mrs. Allen.

When Mr. Allen arrived, he went straight to Jamie. "Son, you are no longer in danger from the hoodlums. Your oil painting is in your care again." He unwrapped it so Jamie could see it. "You see, only the corner of the frame is damaged a bit. The hoodlums are in the hands of the law. We can fix the damage done to the frame. From now on, we have only happy things to do."

"Oh, what happy things, Mr. Allen?"

"In the morning, you must roll out early. We are going to break camp here. We are all going out to our own land where we shall settle in the Northwest Territory."

"Oh, Mr. Allen, I can hardly wait to see our new land. I am so thankful you found Mother's oil painting."

"Jamie, dear, we are all thankful that you were rescued from that dreadful cave. Through this experience, we have had our first relationship with the Indians," Grandma Nelson said. "Yes, we are grateful, too, that the picture of our beloved first president has been returned."

"I'll sure try to keep it safe, as I had promised Mother. Sir, I hope Pa can find us on our new land."

"Jamie, some day your pa is going to be found and may want to settle land next to ours."

Panther

Dawn arrived beautiful and clear. Jamie's chores of caring for the horses, cattle, and chickens were finished before he ate a hurried breakfast.

How exciting to realize they would see their own new land that very day. "Mr. Allen, do you know how far from here your land lies?" Jamie asked.

"Yes, Jamie, we judge it to be about four-and-a-half miles. There are a few little hills and one quite long. The long one is not steep. We have to cross a good-sized stream and go through some wooded areas before we get there," answered Mr. Allen.

"I guess you want me to herd the cattle like I did when we left Virginia?"

"Yes, and keep an eye on the beauty of this new land as we go along. In another minute or two, we'll be ready."

Jamie even found his old herding stick. They had already said their farewells to the remaining wagon folk the night before; however, here they all came to see them off. Jamie felt sad to leave his friends. They had been together ever since they left Virginia, except when they came down the Ohio River. He wanted to ask when he might see his friends again, but Mr. Allen seemed too busy to be bothered by questions.

Jamie was anxious to get started, too. Mr. Hillis walked along with him for a ways. He said they would probably see them soon when they were ready to put up their log cabin.

The Allens, Grandma Nelson, and Jamie were not alone. The Reeves, in their wagon, and Mr. Busby, Mr. Allen's hired man, were going, too. The Reeves had claimed land next to the Allens.

As he had done through the journey from Virginia, Mr. Busby rode and led the extra horses. Mr. Busby had been a soldier in the Revolutionary War and often slept in his amy bedroll. He was as anxious as anyone else to make a claim in the Northwest Territory. He was hoping to find a wife.

"I wonder if I could find my way back to Marietta," Jamie said to himself. He would have to go once in a while to see if his pa had arrived in Ohio or if anyone may have seen him.

It seemed they had traveled quite a while when they came to the big stream they had to cross. It surely reminded all of them of the time they had crossed the Potomac. Jamie could almost feel again that terrible force which had pulled him under the water. He was thankful when he was able to walk through the stream.

From the stream they went up the long, but not steep, hill then through more beautiful woods. In a clearing, they turned to the right and a little further, they went up on a slight rise. Mr. Allen stopped and called loudly, "We are home! This is our new land."

The women jumped out of the wagons, hugged their husbands, then each other. Jamie noticed the women had tears in their eyes. *I guess my mother would have done the same thing*, thought Jamie. *Oh, Pa, why can't you be here with me?*

Jamie could hardly wait to help get the cattle and horses tied so he could run and see everything.

While the men set up camp, Jamie ran into the nearby woods. Surely, he thought, it was filled with treasures. He spread out his arms and ran as fast as he could. What a free and happy feeling he had as he heard the breeze whistle past his ears!

He saw a branch on the ground that looked like a gun. He picked it up, and throwing it over his shoulder, sang "Yankee Doodle" as loud as he could. He was so thrilled and happy. He pretended to be a soldier on parade.

The magic of the moment suddenly vanished when he heard a low growl, which surely was from a wild animal.

His heart started beating loudly in his ears. He slowly looked around and saw nothing to fear. He felt that eyes were watching him. Carrying the stick, now like a club, he made a quick retreat back to their newly made camp.

It felt strange, and scary, to return to only two wagons. Yes, he missed the secure feeling of the other wagon people. Some of them had already gone down the Ohio River to Kentucky.

The Reeves' and Allens' wagons had been placed in the clearing near the woods, supposedly safer that way from summer storms.

Sitting and leaning back against a tree Mr. Allen said, "We surely have found a corner of heaven on this old earth. Just look at these majestic trees!"

Trying to forget the scare he had had, Jamie asked, "Would you show me which is the oak tree?"

"Sure, Jamie, just let me cool off a bit. How about bringing us some of that wonderful cold spring water? Bring the ladle along and pass it around," said Mr. Allen.

The spring was down a little hill, near their camp.

"Certainly, be glad to, Mr. Allen. I'll pass it to the ladies, too."

As Jamie passed the cold, refreshing spring water, he listened to the men talking about the kinds of trees they would cut for the cabin and the furniture. He thought of the wonderful wood he would find for his carving.

"Jamie, did you see something in the woods that frightened you?" asked Grandma Nelson. "I heard you singing, then you came back here carrying a big stick. Were you pretending to be hunting?"

Jamie wanted to tell them what he had heard, but he was afraid they would think it was his imagination. All the way back he had been so frightened he was sure his hair was standing on end, and they would have noticed. "I was pretending to be a soldier," he said.

"Boys will be boys," said Mr. Allen. "I'm going to get a dog for you as soon as we can find a good one."

"Thank you, Mr. Allen, I sure do want one."

Mr. Allen recalled seeing a fish in the stream they had crossed. He asked how they would like fish for supper. Everyone was very much in favor.

Before the men left, they cut firewood and made sure the animals were securely tethered. They built a good fire so that the fish could be cooked as soon as they returned.

Mr. Allen said, "Jamie, I'm sure the womenfolk will need help in getting their cooking things ready. Would you stay and help them?"

Though Jamie was disappointed he said, "Sure, Mr. Allen, but please let me go next time."

When Mr. Reeves asked if the women thought they'd cut enough firewood, Grandma Nelson said, "We've enough wood to cook by for several days. Go on and catch us some big fish."

As the men rode off, Jamie listened to the sounds of the horses and men fading into the distance. He listened carefully to the sounds from the woods. He heard no animal growling; instead, birds were singing and insects were humming. The women were stretched out on the grass, except for Grandma Nelson who sat in her rocking chair.

"Won't this be a beautiful place for our homes, a cabin now and a big, two-story house later?" Mrs. Allen said dreamily.

Suddenly Mrs. Allen sat up. "I'm sure I heard the call of a panther!"

"I heard that, too. Oh, Precious Lord, help us. I hope not!" cried Mrs. Reeves.

"Jamie, let's gather more of these fallen branches and put them with the firewood. We can be cleaning up our building site as well as gathering wood," said Mrs. Allen. She stared into the woods and tried not to be scared.

Also trying not to show fear, Jamie said, "Is this where we are going to build our cabin?"

"Yes, won't it be great to have a real roof over our heads and even four good walls around us?"

Jamie was so worried about that wild animal, which he knew now was a panther, he could think of nothing else to say. How he wished they had those four walls now.

The panther cry sounded much nearer next time.

Mrs. Reeves went to her wagon to get her baby son. She asked Grandma Nelson to hold him. "I think we must build up our fire for protection," said Mrs. Reeves as she carefully placed the now crying baby in Grandma Nelson's arms. "He seems to know we are in danger."

"You'd better make a circle of fire around us," Grandma Nelson suggested. She could not stop the baby from crying and worried that his cries attracted the panther.

"What shall we do if the panther comes closer?" wailed Mrs. Allen. "They even attack horses and cattle."

Furiously, they added wood to the fire and built a ring of fire around them. They were nearly out of big branches. Mrs. Allen yelled, "Jamie, you must get those branches over there."

"How?" he yelled back. "I can't get outside of this ring of fire!"

"You can, and you must! Here, I'll push this branch aside enough for you to jump over. Pick up as much as you can in one sweep and get back in here. We may even have to burn the rocking chair," Mrs. Allen answered.

"Oh, please," cried Grandma Nelson, "not my rocking chair. Oh, Lord help us, and make this baby stop crying!"

"I see the panther standing by that big tree!" Grandma Nelson screamed as she pointed.

Jamie's heart beat loudly in his ears. He broke into a sweat. Almost blinded with smoke and fear, Jamie did as Mrs. Allen asked. Out of the circle he jumped. When he started to pick up the branches, his arms felt as if they would not move. As he bent over he could just imagine the panther attacking him from behind. Quickly he filled his arms and jumped back inside the ring of fire. Mrs. Allen closed the gap with a burning branch.

Shaking too hard to move, Jamie looked up. The panther had gone up into a tree, and his tail was switching furiously back and forth. He looked as if he were ready to jump into their midst!

The horses were neighing and trying to break free. The cattle were jumping and bawling. The baby was still crying loudly. With coughs from smoke and tears of fear, and bathed in perspiration, the women and Jamie kept the fire blazing around them.

The men, while fishing, saw there was more smoke from their camp-site than there should be, so they agreed to return. Nearing camp they shot their guns into the air to let their wives know they were coming.

As they rode into the clearing, they were alarmed at the sight. Jamie was so relieved to see them. Mrs. Allen called to them and pointing, said "A panther! He ran when he heard your gunshots."

It was quickly decided that Mr. Busby would remain with the women and help Jamie gather more branches to burn. He took all of the fish and dropped them into a bucket. He stood ready with his gun should the panther come in sight.

Time seemed to stand still. Jamie noticed no one talked; instead, they each kept their eyes toward the woods and listened. Even the birds and insects stopped singing, apparently disturbed by the smoke and gun-shots. Jamie and the women continued to keep the fire going. Mr. Busby kept watch.

One gunshot, followed by two more, rang through the countryside. Could they have found the panther already?

"Could we be where many panthers live?" asked Mrs. Allen.

"Surely, we must expect these things from this unknown land. Don't you worry. Keep alert to their cries, and let us men know. We will be ready at once to hunt them," answered Mr. Busby.

Soon the two men returned with the body of the panther pulled by a horse. It was a male about seven to eight feet long. Its coat was gray-ish brown, and the underbelly was light in color. How much better they all felt knowing he no longer threatened them.

Though he was a menace, Jamie could not help but admire the beauty of the animal. Maybe one day he could carve one.

"Do you think another panther is still near?" Jamie asked Mr. Busby.

"Yes," Mr. Busby answered. "It is possible, I fear."

Jamie then told them about his having heard the panther in the woods. They assured him that after this, he should let them know imme-diately. And, for their protection, they would continue to keep a good

fire going. The men would take turns being on guard during the night.

When Mrs. Reeves was able to take her son from Grandma Nelson, he stopped his crying. It was as if he knew of the terrible danger they were in from the panther. He then sensed that it was, for the time being, over.

The cattle, horses, birds, and insects calmed down, and once again, the birds were singing. They, too, must have sensed the danger.

The women prepared a delicious fish dinner. Mrs. Allen told the men how bravely Jamie had gone outside the ring of fire to pick up more branches and how hard they all had worked to protect themselves.

Jamie was glad he could do what was asked of him. Maybe by the time he found his pa, he could tell him of this and other acts of bravery.

Jamie wondered how he might be able to see a panther close enough to see how to carve it and yet be at a safe distance from it. What a wonderful place they had found, so full of wonders and adventure.

Log Cabin

"Wake up, wake up quick!" Grandma Nelson called. "There's a wagon coming; I can hear it."

"Oh-oh-I'm awake," answered Jamie as he sat up rubbing his eyes. While he pulled on his pants, he thought, *It's finally here! The day of the cabin raising. We've waited two months.*

Grandma Nelson called again, "Hurry, you must be ready to show people where to park their wagons. Everybody we know in Ohio will be here, and even some we don't know."

Jumping down from the wagon Jamie heard the morning "cheer–up" of a robin and the creak and rattle of the first arriving wagon. He smelled the freshly turned earth at the building site and saw the beautiful morning star shining brightly in the clear sky.

The first to arrive were the Harrisons. Jamie showed them where to leave their wagon and helped Mrs. Harrison carry her baskets of food to the tables. He silently hoped she had brought some of her famous apple tarts.

More families, some with sleepy little ones, arrived. Each provided food for their own needs and plenty more to share.

Lumber from the Allen longboat, which was built in Pittsburgh and on which they had ridden down the Ohio River to Marietta, had been delivered to their building site soon after they claimed their land.

"I see Mr. Allen is well–prepared for the building," Mr. Harrison observed.

"Yes," said Jamie, "I helped him and Mr. Reeves mark the trees to be cut and find boulders for the cornerstones. Yesterday, both Mr. Allen and Mr. Reeves worked all afternoon setting the cornerstones in the ground so they would support level floor and walls. Mr. Busby worked at clearing the land."

"Very good. I'll get my tools," said Mr. Harrison.

The arrival of wagons was almost constant. Jamie was kept very busy showing them where to leave their wagons and helping carry baskets of food to the tables.

Jamie watched and listened to Jeremiah Gibson, who had directed the building of several cabins. He knew who was best at cutting, preparing, or shaping logs. Each man assigned a job seemed pleased and went immediately to work. The older boys worked with their fathers.

Jamie asked, "What does shaping the log mean?"

Mr. Gibson explained that shaping was done near the log ends so that one fits tightly into the next log. He winked at Jamie and said, "Any man can shape a log, but few can do it well. We want this cabin to be well-built."

"Pa and I will want a well-built cabin, too, Mr. Gibson," said Jamie.

"Don't you live with the Allens?" asked Mr. Gibson.

"Yes, but only until I find my pa. You see, he is a soldier and on duty somewhere out west. I'm sure he'll want a log cabin when he gets here," Jamie answered.

"Well, young man, I hope you find him soon. Just let me know when he wants that cabin built," Mr. Gibson said.

When the Hillis family arrived, Mr. Hillis asked Teddy to help his mother with the food baskets.

"Jamie, before I park my wagon, I need to haul my workbench and the already-made shingles to the building site. I'll need your help, with Andrew's, to get my workbench out. I've tools and a bundle of shingles already made," Mr. Hillis said.

"Sure, I'll be glad to help," said Jamie. "I helped build these long tables by setting boards on sawhorses. I helped get all of these logs rolled here for people to sit upon."

Huge fires crackled under tripods supporting large cooking pots. Jamie loved the smell of wood smoke. He noticed that the smoke rose straight up, a good weather sign.

Jamie and the other younger boys had to keep a good supply of wood at hand for the women. It was surprising to see how much wood they had already burned. Mrs. Allen had told him they would need good hot fires early for cooking.

Eight-year-old Benny Harrison was carrying an armload of wood to the pile. Jamie knew he would do a good job. His mother had said she could depend upon him doing well at anything he did since he was six years old.

The air was filled with sounds of chatter from the women and shouts of men to horses and oxen. The call of, "Timber," could often be heard before the mighty crash of a tree to the ground. The scraping of adze to wood and the hammering of pegs also filled the warming summer air.

As Jamie stood watching them chop a tree, he had a hunger pang and remembered he had not eaten breakfast. When he ran back to the wagon, he found Grandma Nelson trying to get her rocking chair out.

"Grandma Nelson, help me find some johnnycake." She watched him stuff his mouth with it. "Now, I'll take your chair and put it where you want it."

During the time that he was helping Grandma Nelson, he felt as if someone were watching him. Sure enough, when he turned his head, the prettiest girl he had ever seen was looking straight at him. Right beside her was Teddy. He was asking her if she wouldn't like one of his mother's apple tarts! The girl turned and smiled at Teddy, thanked him, and refused the tart. Jamie decided he would ask her if she would like to see his favorite fishing spot.

Someone called, "Jamie." He would just have to forget the pretty girl for now. Someone wanted a drink of water, another of Jamie's jobs for the day.

Long before noontime, soft breezes carried the aroma of coffee and roasting meats to all the workers. Jamie felt hungry again already.

"Come here, Jamie," Mr. Estes called. Standing very straight he asked, "Which way does my shadow fall?"

Jamie had a good sense of direction and answered, "Due north. It sure is short, isn't it?"

"Yes," answered Mr. Estes. "In summer, the sun is almost straight over our heads. Now remember to check your shadow around next Christmas and see how different it is then."

The shadow lying due north meant it was high noon. Mr. Estes rang the bell he had used on their wagon train trip to call the folks together.

Workmen started gathering to eat. First, each one washed his hands in one of the two half-barrels. Soap and towels lay on a stump next to the barrels. Buckets of water stood ready to refresh the supply in the barrels.

After what seemed to Jamie a much too long prayer of thanksgiving, the women started serving plates of food. Some of the men would come to eat after this first group had eaten. In the meantime, they would keep working.

Jamie went to make sure the animals had enough water. He ran back to see what was going on at dinner, just in time to see Teddy chewing on a chicken leg and following the pretty girl. Jamie wondered what he could do to get away from him. He knew. He would sit where she would have to wait on him at the table.

When the second shift sat down to eat, the Long Hunter asked, "Jamie, would you like to sit by me?"

"Yes, hold my place." Jamie went to the half–barrel and threw water over his sweaty hands and face. He smoothed down his hair. He didn't dry his hands for the coolness felt good.

Grandma Nelson brought him his and the Long Hunter's plates. He was disappointed that the pretty girl hadn't brought them. When he looked at his plate, he forgot the girl. His plate was heaped with roast pork, baked beans, corn bread, baked sweet potatoes, and an apple tart. In addition to all of what Jamie had were dishes piled with both white potatoes and sweet potatoes, baked beans, rolls and sliced breads, meats, pickle, boiled eggs, pies, and cakes.

When the men had eaten and gone, Grandma Nelson said to Jamie, "I believe I saw you watching a very pretty girl. Do you really like her?"

"Yes, I do," Jamie said and felt his face grow very warm. "She is the first girl I have really liked."

Grandma Nelson sent Jamie to ask the pretty girl for a cup of coffee. He learned her name was Mary Beth. She was even prettier up close.

By the time Jamie returned to the building site, men could no longer lift the heavy logs to the high walls. They made wooded skids on which the log was placed. Ropes around the log were fastened to a pair of horses on the other side of the wall. At a given signal, the horses pulled the log up the skids. Men handling the log pushed at the same time as it was pulled up the skids. Other men fitted the new log into the highest logs in the wall.

Building the "catted" chimney would come after the walls were up. It would be built of stones held together with clay. The clay was mixed with small stones and sticks. Jamie hoped they would let him help smear the clay inside of the chimney.

Mr. Brackney asked, "Jamie, how about helping me steady this pole? All you have to do is help me keep it balanced and in place."

"Of course I'll help you," Jamie answered.

"Now, don't be nervous, just keep it from moving."

Jamie saw little two–year–old Michael Pruitt come toddling along. Surely someone would see him. Jamie could not move and felt he shouldn't yell for fear it would jar the pole.

As the other men stepped back to sight the pole position, Jamie saw that little Michael kept coming closer. Oh, please, someone see him and get him out of the way in case this pole should fall. Mr. Brackney had a sudden sneezing fit. The pole wavered a bit. Jamie held on as hard as he could. The pole swayed.

Jamie yelled, "I can't hold it." Neither he nor Mr. Brackney could keep it from falling. It hit the earth with a mighty boom, just missing little Michael Pruitt.

The men who saw what happened were in shock. The first one able to move was Michael's father. He ran, picked up the frightened child, and cradled him in his arms as he carried him to his mother.

Too weak to move, Jamie started crying. "To think I was supposed to hold the pole from moving. I couldn't and it almost hit little Michael."

Mr. Brackney put his arm around Jamie and said, "Son, it was my fault that the pole gave way. We must be thankful that the child escaped injury."

Jamie thought, *I don't want anybody to call me "son." I need my real Pa. He wouldn't have let this happen.*

After such a scare, the men could hardly move themselves to get back to work. Every minute of daylight was precious in order to finish the cabin that day. Back to work they went. Jamie sat and watched for a while.

When the ridgepole was in place and the ceiling of the cabin in, it was time to carry shingles up the ladder to the roofers. Four men worked on each side of the roof.

After seeing Mrs. Allen and Mrs. Harrison crawl up the ladder to the loft in order to hand shingles up through the roof beams, Jamie picked up an armful of shingles and started up the ladder. The steps were wide apart. He was three steps up and looked down. He was so far away from the floor! He was filled with fear. He stopped and held on tight to the roughly hewn ladder.

I cannot go any higher, he thought with surprise. *I'd better go back down before Teddy sees me.* To go down was as scary as going up. He had watched Teddy, Jim, and Andrew go right up carrying shingles. What was he going to do?

If he didn't go down the ladder he'd have to sleep there. That thought amused him enough to take the first step down. He was shaking like a leaf, but he made it down one very long step after the other. He made it before Teddy saw him.

Jamie found Grandma Nelson and told her, "Grandma Nelson, I can't seem to go up the ladder to the loft. I was halfway up and was so scared I couldn't go higher."

"You do have a problem. Haven't you ever climbed the high branches in a tree?"

"No," he answered, "I've always climbed the branches near the ground."

"Let's not tell anyone. Take the men some good cold water to drink. I'll get my old basket. We'll go near the river to dig up some clay for the chinking." When their basket was heavy, they carried it back along the narrow path to the building site.

Arriving at the cabin, they just stood and looked. Only this morning, there had been woods only. Now there was a nearly finished cabin.

All of the shingles were on. Jamie saw how the second row of shingles covered where shingles came together in the first row. "I'll know how when Pa and I build our cabin. Look, Grandma Nelson, why are the shingles along the ridgepole higher on one side?"

"They tell me that is so the water sheds from them and does not leak inside. Those three boards they are putting across the shingles are somehow tied to the beams underneath and hold the shingles down in case of strong winds," Grandma Nelson said.

Two men were building the door. They had already cut the doorway hole and framed it. Jamie asked, "Mr. Black, how can you build the door so it can stay shut or swing open?"

Mr. Black had been hammering wooden pegs into the door. After he hammered a board across the bottom of the upright boards, he pegged a place across near the top. "Now, son, if you can hand me a couple more pegs, we'll show you how the door works."

Jamie asked, "Did you make all of those pegs?"

"Sure did. We make all we can on rainy days when we can't work outside. The boys help us, too."

"Why is that peg sticking up there?" Jamie asked as he pointed to a peg sticking out of what would be the top of the door.

"Look down at the door sill. See that spot we've marked. We'll auger that out and put in the bottom peg already on the door. Stand back and watch how we hold the door in place and mark where that top peg goes into the frame," Mr. Black instructed.

"I wish I could help you do that," Jamie said.

"Thanks, son, I'd let you auger out the hole in the top of the frame, but you are not tall enough, and, besides, it must be perfectly straight up and down."

Jamie next went to see if he could help with the chimney. It was nearly finished.

Sun shadows were getting long, telling everyone the day was nearly done. So was the log cabin.

Mr. Estes rang the bell, and all of the adults gathered in the twenty-by-thirty-foot Allen cabin. The puncheon floor easily supported them. How happy Jamie and everyone else was with their accomplishment of the day.

After a date was set for their next party, the sound of building changed to the sounds of hitching up teams of wagons, calls of farewell, the creaking of wagons, and happy voices as they drove away.

When the people had gone, the chores were done, and they had eaten, it was time to bring his bedding into the cabin. Jamie's fear of heights lessened when he and Mr. Busby carried bedding to the loft. Mr. Busby was one step behind Jamie as he went up. Jamie did not look back and panic at the height. Going down the ladder, Mr. Busby went down a step before Jamie, so he again did not fear the height nearly as much.

Mr. Allen said he knew of a good friend, back in Virginia, who was also afraid of heights. He had made himself get over it so that he could go into his barn loft. Jamie must try to get over it, too.

The Reeves family and Mr. Busby would sleep in the Allens' cabin until their cabins were built.

No more sleeping in what now looked like a small covered wagon. As he lay on his bedding, Jamie wished his mother could see their cabin. A smile came with the thought of Mary Beth.

Wrapped in the warm smell of freshly cut wood, Jamie saw a bright star shining through the yet uncovered window. He made a wish that soon he would find his pa. He could see himself and Pa sitting in front of a fireplace in a cabin just like this one.

He was thankful the little Pruitt boy wasn't hurt. He would try hard to get over his fear of heights. He was soon asleep.

Contest

Jamie held the wooden top between his thumb, on the bottom, and a finger, on top. Turning it slowly, he checked to see if it were evenly shaped. Yes, a little bit more in one spot would make it better balanced. Taking great care to shave a little bit more, he was unaware of the soft summer sounds that surrounded him.

The constant toot on a whistle caught his attention.

"Edwin, why are you blowing that whistle?" Jamie asked as Edwin joined him.

"I like to hear it. Thanks, Jamie, for giving it to me. Mrs. Allen said you probably made it of willow wood," Edwin answered.

"Yes, see those trees down there by the pond? That's where I found the wood for it. Do you know, Edwin, I've been in Ohio for a whole year. We didn't even have a cabin for several weeks after we found our land."

"Did you know me when you came here?" Edwin asked.

"No, you came here before we did. Has anyone told you that your mother is getting a baby while you are staying with us?" Jamie asked.

"No, really! Mamma asked me how I would like a sister but didn't say she was going to get one. Do you think I'll like a sister?"

"I don't know, for I never had one. Are you going to school next year?" Jamie asked.

"Yes, I think so. I can't wait to see the new school building when we go this week," Edwin answered.

Eyeing the top carefully again, Jamie said, "I think the top is finished. Let's go back to the cabin so I can spin it on the smooth floor."

As they entered the cabin Jamie handed the top to Grandma Nelson. She looked it over and said, "A beautiful job, Jamie. I guess you are ready for the string I promised."

Grandma Nelson and Mrs. Allen came to watch the top's first spin.

They watched in awe and silence as it spun merrily across the floor. When it toppled over, they clapped and cheered Jamie for the fine work he had done.

"Jamie, how would you like your top stained with berry juice?" asked Grandma Nelson.

"It would really look like a store–bought one. The other day, when I saw Teddy Hillis, he asked what I was taking to the dedication. He said he was taking a whistle he had made. When I told him I was making a top to spin in the contest, he laughed and told me that an awkward thing like that would fall over. I would never get a prize on a piece of junk."

"Edwin, go down where you boys picked raspberries and bring a handful back to me," Grandma Nelson said.

Mrs. Nelson gave Edwin a cup and away he ran to get berries.

Grandma Nelson asked Jamie to start unraveling a sock. The socks were too worn out to mend. She had another one there for Edwin. "When he gets back with the berries, he can unravel the other one while I stain your top."

Both boys watched Grandma Nelson stain the top an even blue-red color.

"That color is so beautiful, every eye watching the contest will be on your top, Jamie," encouraged Mrs. Allen.

"I must win the contest, especially since Teddy said my top was a piece of junk," said Jamie.

"I see that we have quite a pile of yarn here," said Grandma Nelson. "While you finish unraveling your sock, Edwin, I want Jamie to find a round, smooth rock about an inch big." She showed him with her fingers.

Grandma Nelson rolled the yarn into a ball while Jamie looked for exactly the right size stone. Satisfied he had found it, he took it to Grandma Nelson.

Jamie asked, "Is this what you want? Edwin, you sure are slow with that sock. Just pull the yarn."

Grandma Nelson reminded Jamie that Edwin was younger and smaller than Jamie.

"Oh, Jamie, this will make a dandy ball," Grandma Nelson said as she took the stone. "Now boys, watch how to make a ball."

She started winding the yarn tightly round and round the rock. It was really getting big. She handed it to Jamie.

"Look, Edwin, we can play ball," Jamie said.

"No, I want you to tell me if it fits and feels good in your hand. Is that a good size for you?" Grandma Nelson asked.

"Yes, it is great. Come on, Edwin, let's play ball."

"No, not yet boys. You see it needs a covering." She had a nice piece of deer skin. She smoothed the skin over the ball until it fit, then she sewed it on. When she was finished, she handed Jamie a smooth, firm ball.

"It is your own ball to keep. Don't lose it, and have lots of fun with it."

Hugging Grandma Nelson, Jamie said, "This is the most wonderful ball I've ever seen. The only one I ever had was a sheep's bladder filled with air."

Jamie went to look at his top before going out with the ball. It was a beautiful color and nearly dry.

When the boys came back from playing with the ball, Mrs. Allen asked, "Jamie, you have several things you can take to the school dedication program, don't you? Do you have them ready?"

"Just about. I'm going to make a box for my top."

"Mother and I are going to take some of our handwork."

Jamie said, "My carvings are ready. I am going to practice spinning my top. I sure do want to win that contest. I'll show Teddy what my top can do. Only two days left to practice."

"Well, enough of the school dedication talk for now. You must be getting your chores done," Mrs. Allen told him.

The day for the school dedication dawned damp and foggy. The fog soon cleared after the sun came up. *Nothing must ruin my topspinning*, thought Jamie. They jostled along in the wagon carrying food raised in their garden and things they had made.

Mary Beth and Jamie's other friends would be there. He could hardly wait to see the new school building. In a couple of weeks school would begin.

When they passed the new church, Jamie knew the school was very near, so he jumped out of the wagon and ran ahead. The school was so very tall and big and inviting.

Men had set up plank tables on sawhorses. As people arrived, they placed their handwork and homemade dolls and toys on the tables. Some of the men were busily marking locations for the running race, wrestling, and other contests.

"I'm glad I've practiced and practiced spinning my top," Jamie said to himself. He saw three other boys with tops.

While placing his carvings on the display table, August Lauer asked Jamie, "Where is your top, Jamie? I heard that you had painted it. Don't you know that the paint will make it heavier and hold it down?"

Jamie wanted to tell August to get out of his way, but instead he said, "My top is not going to be seen until the contest. I'm sure its finish will not slow it down. Did you bring one?"

"Yes, and you are going to see how well a good top can spin in a contest with junkers like yours."

Teddy probably told him I made my top, and it doesn't even spin, Jamie thought to himself. *Well, I made it as good as I can, and now, when the contest starts, I must toss it just right. What will Mary Beth think of me if I don't win that contest?*

The girls had made dolls of corn, using the silk for hair and clothes made of husks. Other dolls were made with scraps of material and stuffed with saw dust or bits of cloth. Some doll clothing had been knitted or crocheted.

One of the boys had carved a doll cradle; another, a bench. Others had made sleds, a cart, a pair of ice skates, whistles, and carved birds and animals. Wooden pegs for building were included. Beneath the table, in homemade cages, was a crow and a huge pet rabbit. Dogs had to be left at home.

Mr. Estes announced that the day's contests would start with a runner's race. The wrestling match would be next, then the topspinning contest would be held on the school entrance platform. Jamie didn't even hear the rest of the announcements, for he was so nervous about his top.

Everyone, even the women who had been busy inside the schoolhouse, gathered around to watch each contest. There was Mary Beth! Jamie thought, *I almost wish she wouldn't watch. No, I wish she would. I am certain that Teddy won't be in the contest, but he will probably watch and make comments on what happens.*

At the gunshot, the runners started. They had to make six laps around. All took off at great speed. Too soon, Clem Miller turned his ankle and dropped out. Short–legged Tom Brown and George Landes were far behind. The last lap brought screams from everyone, for Will Estes and Ed Foreman were neck and neck. Will was able to touch the flagpole just seconds before Ed.

It seemed that listing the rules for the wrestling took forever, but when the gun was shot, they were punching and rolling until Martin Clark stood as a winner. They gave them two more rounds, but Martin won the first two.

And now the very minute had come to spin his top. Jamie took his place at the school entrance platform. Each contestant had a corner. Jamie blew any dust off of his corner. The crowd pushed up so close they had to be asked to step back. Jamie wished they wouldn't use a gun for the starter. He was nervous anyway. He felt he could hardly breathe.

He and his top were ready for the gun signal.

Bang.

He tossed the top out.

It spins sure and beautiful, Jamie thought.

The crowd was so quiet all that could be heard was the spinning of the tops on the new wooden platform.

"Oh, no, no!" Jamie called as his top edged into a crack. "Move out of that crack! Keep spinning! Help, you can't quit now! Get away from that crack!"

The noble top bent one direction and down it fell.

At the second signal, all four tops were spinning again. Jamie could hardly bear it when he saw the top edging toward that crack. He literally held his breath until his was the last top spinning.

He broke out in a sweat all over. *Now, our third spin gives me a chance to win*, Jamie thought as he wiped his sweaty palms on his pants.

The third signal sounded, and all the tops were spinning again. Jamie leaned way over trying to persuade the top to move from the crack. The top seemed to have a will of its own. Jamie was soon aware that only one other top was spinning, and people were yelling.

Out of the corner of his eye, he saw that the other top spinning belonged to August Lauer. Jamie could hardly take a breath. He wanted to blow on his, anything to keep it going longer. "Please keep spinning." He couldn't even look at the other top, but he thought it was slowing down, and fell.

"Keep spinning, my beautiful top, a little bit longer." It did, but already the crowd was clapping and calling his name until he couldn't even remember what happened afterward. He did remember clearly the big smile Mary Beth gave him and a wonderful whole new ball of string they gave him for a prize.

Though never listed as a contest, setting her food on the table was the pride of every lady and girl present. And, there, too, was Mary Beth.

After dropping his ball of string into Mrs. Allen's basket, Jamie wanted so much to speak to her.

"Mary Beth, I saw you before the topspinning contest."

"Oh, Jamie," she said with that big beautiful smile. "Your top looks like a store-bought one and spins like magic. Congratulations on winning the contest."

"Well, I hoped you would be there. Thanks. I'm really pleased with that top," Jamie said shyly. "Did you make this cake, Mary Beth?"

"No, my mother did. I made this maple sugar taffy," she said as she passed it to him. "I'd like to learn how to spin a top."

"I'll be glad to teach you, maybe this afternoon. I'm going to watch the broad jumping now. Mmmm, good taffy!"

When everyone was called into the new schoolhouse for dinner, they all sang a thanksgiving hymn. Dinner was a wonderful display of meats, vegetables, peach pies, and cakes loaded with frosting.

After eating, the men all gathered on the grass under the trees. Jamie loved to listen to their tales of Indian encounters, narrow escapes from wild animals, and tremendously big fish caught in the Muskingham River.

Young girls helped their mothers and listened as they shared ideas on cooking, childbearing, and child upbringing. Smaller children played singing games such as "London Bridge" and "Farmer in the Dell."

Jamie was dreaming of Mary Beth when he heard Mr. Brackney say, "Jamie, we're going to have some puppies at our house real soon. Would you like one?"

"Yes, please, Mr. Brackney. I would take good care of it. Mr. Allen, could I have one?"

"Of course, Jamie. If you have extra ones, we actually could use two of them. How would you like that, Jamie?"

Mr. Brackney said he didn't know yet how many there would be, but he would have their names on his list.

"Jamie, Mr. Eads told me how interested you are in fiddles. He knows where we can get one. Would you like to have a fiddle?" asked Mr. Pruitt.

"Yes, oh yes, I would surely like to have one. Maybe I could even play at the next square dance."

All the men laughed at Jamie's enthusiasm and encouraged him.

"You know, folks, the sun shadows tell me that we'd better get our next get-together planned. There is much to be done before sundown," Mr. Harrison cautioned. "Already the days are getting shorter."

The men joined the women inside the new schoolhouse.

They decided their next get–together would be next Saturday in William Clark's new barn. There they should have recitations, singing, dancing, and maybe even some drama and mime.

It didn't take long for each family to gather and pack their own things into their wagons. The countryside was filled with sounds of people calling farewell and families chatting and laughing together while commands to their horses blended with the sound of wheels turning on the August-dry, dusty roadway. Blue gentians growing along the roadside were almost white with the dust.

As they rode home, Jamie's mind raced with the many ways he could use his very own string. To think, he might get a puppy and get a fiddle, too.

Edwin dropped over on Jamie's lap, for he had fallen asleep. Jamie wished Grandma Nelson could take him but didn't want to awaken him.

How could anyone be happier than I am? If only Pa could be with me, everything would be perfect.

Arriving at the cabin, Edwin awakened and helped Jamie feed the chickens. They ate some leftovers, and Jamie, with Edwin, soon was in bed.

First Violin Lesson

Pa might find me fiddling for a barn dance, Jamie thought as he walked through the woods carrying his violin. The hollow feeling came into his chest as it always did when he thought about his father. All the way here, from Virginia to Ohio, they had looked, and no trace of him was found.

"I must watch where I'm going, for it is not easy to find my violin teacher's house. I wish I could have my own horse."

Arriving at his teacher's cabin, he was greeted by a short, jolly Mr. Anders. "Good morning, Jamie, come in. Is this your puppy?"

"Yes, sir, it is. Come here, Spot. He wanted to come along in the worst way. He promised me he would wait outside while I have my lesson," Jamie said.

Once inside Jamie found the cabin dark after the bright sunshine outdoors.

"Here, Jamie, take this seat near my chair," said Mr. Anders.

Jamie felt afraid to sit so close to his teacher, but he did as he was told.

"Here is my violin," Jamie said as he proudly opened the case.

Mr. Anders picked up the violin. "This is a beautiful instrument," he said, as he turned the violin this way and that. He even tried to see inside of it. Jamie noticed the backs of his hands had shiny red hairs as he gently handled his violin.

Holding the violin in an upright position on his knee, Mr. Anders said, "I know you are anxious to get started. As I name the parts of the violin I want you to point and name them after me. These are the shoulders."

Of course, Jamie thought, *they are under the neck just like mine. And the bridge looks like a bridge*. He wondered if he could ever handle the violin as easily as Mr. Anders.

Turning the violin around, his teacher said, "You will see the front and back are like the belly and the back."

A knock sounded on the door, and a voice called, "Uncle Paul, do you have company?"

Oh my, Jamie thought, *that surely sounded like Mary Beth. I wish I could hide. I don't want her to watch my very first lesson. Still, I'd like to see her.*

"Excuse me, young man." He handed the violin to Jamie. "I'll speak to my caller."

As he went to the door he called out, "Mary Beth, my dear child, could you come back a bit later? I was just starting to give Jamie his first violin lesson."

"Yes, Mamma said I should not bother you if you were giving a lesson. Could this cute dog belong to Jamie?"

"Yes, it is his," said Mr. Anders.

"May I just come in and speak to Jamie?" Mary Beth asked.

In she came. "Hello, Jamie."

He wanted to speak to her so badly, but he didn't know what to say. He became very nervous and squirmed in his chair. He stood up, then said, "I heard you say you like my puppy."

"Yes, it is such a cute dog."

"Mary Beth, I didn't know you lived near here. I'm glad to see you," Jamie muttered.

"Yes, I must run along. I am happy to know that you are going to play the violin. Will you play it at school?"

Mr. Anders said, "Yes, maybe he will, but we must get on with the lesson, for I've another student coming after Jamie."

"Good bye, Jamie, I'll see you at school."

Jamie could feel that his face had become real hot. The way Mr. Anders looked at him, he knew he was blushing.

"I didn't know you and Mary Beth were such good friends," Mr. Anders commented. "She is my sister's daughter and a lovely girl. Now, let me think, where were we?"

It was hard for Jamie to get his mind back on the violin. "You had just pointed out that the violin's rounded shape is called the belly in the front, and it has a back," Jamie said.

"To be sure. The sound comes out of the inside through the F holes. Inside, under the bridge, you will see a post called a sound post."

Leaving the violin on Jamie's lap, his teacher named and pointed to the tailpiece, strings, fingerboard, and peg box.

Jamie easily named all of the parts.

Mr. Anders seemed well pleased. He then said, "The strings are tuned a fifth apart, or each string is five tones above the one below."

Jamie watched Mr. Anders go to the reed organ where he stood and pumped one pedal as he played the G, D, A, and E tones for the pitches, or tones of the strings.

He asked, "Jamie, would you sing those tones back to me? Just sing them on *la*."

Jamie sang them back, and Mr. Anders seemed well pleased.

Mr. Anders came back and sat down. He plucked the strings on the violin and asked Jamie if they needed tuning."

"Yes, I can tune them. Mr. Reeves already taught me how."

Looking sternly at Jamie, Mr. Anders said, "Young man, I am your teacher and no one else."

I guess it was wrong to say Mr. Reeves taught me, Jamie thought. *Oh, Mr. Anders surely hates me*, Jamie feared.

Plucking the strings again, Mr. Anders asked, "Are they in tune?"

Jamie knew they needed tuning, but he was not able to answer. He sure hoped Mary Beth wasn't listening. She was even prettier than she was when school was out last spring.

"How can we get the strings up to pitch?" Mr. Anders seemed aggravated with Jamie.

"I know, I know," said Jamie, and he started turning a peg.

"Stop! Stop, stop that!" hollered Mr. Anders.

A horribly loud and sickening pop sound filled the room, and a loose end of string flew.

"Oh, you've broken it! Where in the world do you expect to get another string?" Mr. Anders shrieked. "You must never turn a string peg without listening to the pitch." His face was as red as fire.

Jamie's heart was pounding loudly in his ears. Hot tears rolled down both cheeks. Between sobs he managed to say, "I am sorry. I don't know where to get strings."

"I'll look in your case," said Mr. Anders. "There's no place to get strings out here in the wilderness. Lucky for you. Old Mr. Foxworthy brought some extra strings, even two of the E string that you broke. We have to wait until they are shipped here from Pittsburgh. Old Mr. Foxworthy definitely was a fine old gentleman, and, incidentally, a fine violinist. He took good care of his things. You must learn to do the same."

"I am very sorry," Jamie managed to say in almost a whisper.

"It must not happen again. Watch carefully how to put a new string on your violin." He talked as he worked.

"You must listen to the pitch as you turn the peg. When I get this string put into place I will have to tune it. You will find that this new string will go out of pitch easily for a while. Mr. Reeves may have his way of tuning, but you must learn my method of tuning."

As this point, Jamie's heart was still pounding so loudly he thought surely Mr. Anders could hear it.

When the new string was in place, Mr. Anders played the strings and brought them up to pitch. "You must not try to tune this way at first. I'll show you later how a beginner should tune his strings."

Jamie noticed Mr. Anders just sat and took a big deep breath before he went on with the lesson. His face was changing from an almost black red to a natural color. He suggested Jamie watch how the pitch changed when he placed a finger on the string to shorten its vibrating length. He then played Mozart's theme, "Baa, Baa, Black Sheep."

Jamie could feel Mr. Anders looking at him very closely, then he asked Jamie to sing along with him.

The second time Mr. Anders played the song, Jamie was barely able to get a sound out. He had already dried his face of tears. He tried and soon was able to sing the song.

Mr. Anders placed the violin under Jamie's chin. "Now press up on it with your left shoulder. Let the fingerboard rest in your open left hand. With your right hand, place the frog of the bow so that the thumb is near you. Three of the fingers are on the other side. The little finger will rest on the end of the bow.

"Yes, exactly right, now play just the G string."

With trembling hands, Jamie tried to pull the bow across the big G string, but it hit other strings and a terrible screeching sound resulted.

"Oh, I just cannot do it." Again, Jamie's eyes filled with tears. He wanted so badly to learn to play.

"Young man, with your sense of pitch, you will be playing very soon. Mary Beth will be anxious to hear you play." Taking the violin, Mr. Anders played "Turkey in the Straw" while he vigorously tapped a booted toe. Jamie again felt like the happy boy who had come for his first lesson.

Someone outside whistled the last phrase when Mr. Anders had finished the piece.

Jamie was anxious to see who had come. It was not Mary Beth, but it was the Long Hunter. Jamie was always glad to see him. The Long Hunter called in that he would wait until the lesson was finished.

Mr. Anders asked Jamie to practice playing each string by itself, in rhythm of four beats, the way he then showed him.

"It takes a while to get the feeling of where the strings are in relation to your hand and fingers. You'll get it," said Mr. Anders. "Practice is the only way you will ever be able to play them. Come back for your next lesson when you can play each string in even rhythm. I can see you will play very soon."

Jamie said to himself, *I am not going to let him scare me any more.* He knew his desire to play was stronger than his fear of his teacher. Besides playing for Pa, he must get ready also to play for Mary Beth.

When Jamie carefully replaced the violin and the bow into the wooden case, he went outside with Mr. Anders and spoke to the Long Hunter. Spot came dashing up and jumped happily onto Jamie.

"How soon will you be ready to play for my singing school, Jamie? You've a first-rate teacher in Mr. Anders. He and I knew each other in Baltimore," said the Long Hunter.

"You know, several of us feel that Jamie's father is much more apt to go to St. Louis before he would come to Marietta. The next time we take furs to St. Louis, I am hoping to take Jamie along," said Mr. Adams, the Long Hunter.

"In the meantime, we'll soon have Jamie playing his violin for all kinds of things. Remember, Mary Beth wants you to play for school," added Mr. Anders.

"I want so much to find Pa. How soon would we go to St. Louis?" Jamie asked eagerly.

"It will be months before we have a cargo ready to take out there," answered Mr. Adams.

"I hope I can learn to play real soon. Bye, Mr. Anders and Mr. Adams. I'll be back as soon as my lesson is ready. Come on, Spot."

Jamie looked around for Mary Beth, but he did not see her. He could hardly wait to practice. He had gone quite a way when he saw a very comfortable log. He stopped, sat down on the log, took out his fiddle, and tried to play just the G string.

Spot settled among some wild flowers and listened, but he soon jumped up to chase a butterfly.

Jamie spent many hours practicing for every lesson. He learned not only his assignments but songs he already knew. Barn dance fiddlers took great delight in teaching him their dance music. It was very easy for Jamie.

When school started, he did play often for the children. They loved singing along with his playing.

At times, when Jamie felt lonely for his parents, he found great comfort in playing his violin.

Storm

"Mr. Allen, do you really think Pa will be in St. Louis?" asked Jamie as he and Mr. Allen each carried a bucket of fresh, warm milk from the log barn.

"Yes, Jamie, it has been more than two years since we left Virginia. No one has given us a good lead for finding your father. Several of us feel that your chances of finding him would be better in St. Louis," answered Mr. Allen.

"He might even be at the dock when we get there. Oh, I can hardly wait till we get to St. Louis," said Jamie excitedly.

"Now, don't expect to find him that easily. It's more apt to happen there than here," Mr. Allen advised. "You must keep us informed of your address. We'll continue to keep a watch for him. You can be certain of that."

"I will send you my address and always let you know what I'm doing. I've learned so much from you folks, and I feel at home here with you. I hate to go away, but my longing to be with Pa is stronger than anything else I wish for."

When Jamie crawled into his bed that night he wondered what he would see and do before he found his pa.

It seemed a short night when Jamie was awakened the next morning.

Long before daylight, Jamie and Mr. Reeves said their farewells to the Allens and Grandma Nelson.

"You folks have always been good to me. If I didn't want to find my Pa so badly, I'd not leave you," Jamie told them.

Mrs. Allen reminded Jamie he was always welcome to return and live with them again. She hugged him lovingly, then Grandma Nelson did the same as she handed him a carefully wrapped package and said, "Jamie, you and I have done so much together. I'll really miss you. In this package are socks, underwear, and a new jacket that I made for you."

"Oh, thank you, Grandma Nelson," he said as he hugged her again. "I'll always remember you. There are many happy memories, and you taught me so many things. I can't imagine being without you."

"These clothes may seem large, but the way you're growing, they will soon fit you fine."

"We'll hope you find your pa. I think you will have a greater chance of finding him in St. Louis. Good luck, my boy. I know you are going with good people," Mr. Allen said when he shook hands with Jamie. "Mr. Reeves, I'll come after sunup to get the wagon, as we've planned."

"Yes, sir. I promise you all that I will take good care of Jamie," Mr. Reeves said as he shook hands all around.

At the Marietta, Ohio, dock, a bit of daylight was making it possible to see the mist-covered river. Jamie noticed a strong smell of mud. He shivered with the chilling dampness.

The Long Hunter, whose real name was Adams, and two hunters from Marietta were to be in the lead boat. They were already loading their boat when Jamie and Mr. Reeves arrived. The Hillises joined them a bit afterward.

Mr. Hillis and his son, Teddy, Jamie, and Mr. Reeves were to travel in the second boat.

When unloaded Mr. Reeves drove their wagon a short distance to the livery and walked back to the dock.

While busy arranging their provisions onto the boat Teddy said, "Jamie, looks like you brought everything you own, even your old fiddle."

"Maybe I did bring everything I own," said Jamie.

Mr. Hillis quickly responded, "Teddy, for goodness sake! You know Jamie has to take everything, for he may not return."

"If we could leave him behind, it would be good riddance," muttered Teddy. Then, in a boastful voice so that all could hear, he said "I'm taking a few things I want to trade with the Indians. I figure I can trade my broken pocketknife for something good."

Jamie thought, *I hope someday an Indian will show Teddy how dumb he is instead of how smart he thinks he is.*

"Now, how and where do you except to find any human being that stupid?" his father asked. "Here, take this rope, and get busy and help us tie this canvas down good and tight."

Jamie said, "Oh, Mr. Reeves, you're back already, good. I want to ask you something. How will we know where to camp at night? Do people live along the Ohio River as we go west?"

"Yes, in some places. Especially at Cincinnati, there are many folks, and much going and coming. You sound as if you're not anxious to go, Jamie," said Mr. Reeves.

"I am, but I hope we aren't attacked by warrior Indians."

"Jamie, you are just a baby coward!" said Teddy.

Why does Teddy treat me like a dumb kid? Jamie thought. *He may find out the hard way that not all people are the same.*

"Son, with all of our fine provisions of feed, canvas, and furs, we'll just do as Mr. Adams, the Long Hunter, advises, and we'll be fine. He has made this trip several times. You know we are looking for a market that will pay us higher prices for our furs. We must take good care of our cargo of furs all the way to St. Louis.

Mr. Adams joined them. "Our boat is securely stowed, and we are ready to go. How about you, Jamie? Sounds like you want to back out."

"I really do want to go, but I just wondered what it will be like. Where will we sleep at night?" asked Jamie.

"That is part of the fun. You'll see and learn how to 'rough it' in the wilderness. I think you men will know what to watch for on the river. We won't leave you far behind."

"We are about ready to cast off," said Mr. Hillis. "We'll stay right behind you."

Mr. Reeves and Mr. Hillis would row, which put Jamie and Teddy together. Jamie secretly wished they could go without Teddy. As Grandma Nelson once said, "Sometimes you have to take the bitter with the sweet."

Through the mist they shoved off from shore. Jamie hunched deeper into his jacket and pulled his yarn cap further down over his face to shut out the damp cold.

While casting off, no one said a word. The mist seemed to muffle the sound of the oars. After they found a rhythmic patter of rowing in midstream, Mr. Hillis reminded them to watch for floating logs or other debris. Already the mist was clearing.

Mr. Reeves added, "We need to constantly watch for unfriendly Indians on shore. Also watch for sudden direction change in the river current.

"By the way, Jamie, did you bring your oil painting of George Washington on his horse?"

"What! Surely you didn't bring that old picture! Jamie, you are like an old woman who ties up her belongings into all kinds of bundles," chided Teddy.

"Yes, I did. I promised Mother I would always take good care of it," answered Jamie. I like it and intend to always keep it."

As the mist lifted and the sun felt warm on him, Jamie became very sleepy. Almost as if in a dream, he remembered Mary Beth and the first time he saw her at their house–raising. He was still thrilled to think about how he played his fiddle along with the fiddlers at some barn dances. Tears filled his eyes when he recalled playing for the funeral of Edwin's little brother, Homer. He wondered if he would ever see his schoolmates again.

At midday, when they stopped and went ashore, Jamie realized how tired he was of the boat's motion. It was hard to sit for such a long time. When on shore, he and Teddy raced each other to a big tree and back. Teddy did win, but he had longer legs.

Slices of ham with slices of buttered, homemade bread, apples, and water to drink were their lunch. They ate some of Grandma Nelson's sugar cookies.

When they were ready to travel again, Mr. Hillis asked, "How would you boys like a turn at rowing?"

The boys took their places at the oars. Jamie soon learned it was more work than he had thought. After an hour, the men took the oars again.

Late afternoon, the Long Hunter signaled them to go ashore. Jamie was much relieved, for he was tired of being in the boat.

As they carried their camping supplies to shore, Jamie asked the Long Hunter, "Mr. Adams, how can you camp in the cold, cold winter?"

"Would you like to be a Long Hunter, son?"

Jamie answered, "I don't know. I'll do whatever my pa wants me to do."

"You really believe you'll find your pa?"

"Yes, I am sure, for President Thomas Jefferson said he was somewhere out west."

"Hmmm," Mr. Adams said as he started building a fire. "When it is cold enough to freeze the tail off a 'possum, we make sure we camp out of the wind, and keep the fire going all night."

"I wouldn't want to camp alone," Jamie said.

Before long they had a hot dinner made in a big frying pan. Very tired and sleepy, Jamie crawled into their tent and slept soundly until breakfast. *Why, this is more fun than our covered wagon trip*, he decided.

They expected their second day of travel would be much like the first, except after they passed Cincinnati, there was a stretch of shore to the north which was occupied by hostile Indians.

As they easily moved down the river under a blue sky, Mr. Hillis remarked that the sky ahead looked mighty black. In a few minutes, their blue sky turned very dark. With it came strong icy winds that stung their faces.

Mr. Reeves could hardly be heard above the roaring wind when he turned around and yelled to the boys, "Make sure everything is securely covered and tightly tied down!"

"Look!" Jamie shouted as loud as he could. "Mr. Adams is yelling and waving both arms."

They saw him turn back and head for the forbidden north shore. They followed. By then sharp icy pellets slammed into their faces. Their boat, even after turning away from the wind and almost capsizing in the process, was tossed by the white–capped, churning waters.

"Jamie," yelled Mr. Reeves, "Hold, lay yourself over our cargo, quick!" The men had all they could do to keep the boat from capsizing.

Jamie and Teddy clung to the ropes to help secure their cargo and themselves. Jamie felt his hands being cut by the ropes. He remembered how Grandma Nelson had told him, "When you assure a responsibility, stick to it until it is finished." He held on.

Near shore Mr. Adams shouted, "The current changed. We must get out of here as soon as we can!"

When they had barely touched land, Teddy shouted, "Indians!" and out of the boat he jumped. He ran toward a steep hill covered by trees.

Mr. Hillis yelled, "No, come back, son, come back!"

Teddy just kept on running up the hill.

Teddy, you dunce, thought Jamie, *if you get caught you can blame only yourself.*

In a very short time they heard terrified screams from Teddy. His screams were so horrible that, for the very first time, Jamie felt sorry for him. What horrible things could they be doing to him?

Mr. Adams, gun in hand, motioned Mr. Hillis to get out and follow him up the other side of the bank where Teddy had gone. They each carried loaded guns. Teddy's screams had not stopped.

I hope they don't find the rest of us, Jamie thought.

"Watch out! Here they come!" hollered Mr. Reeves. He tried to hold them off from the boat, but he was overpowered.

Warriors with fierce faces and wearing little but ragged clothing scared Jamie so badly he sat in horror, unable to move.

They hit Mr. Reeves so hard he fell back against Jamie. They swung long, sharp knives to cut the ropes. Ripping the canvas of their cargo, they soon had their arms loaded with the provisions they were stealing.

Mr. Reeves raised his head and tried to get up.

They roughly pawed through the supplies. They had taken Mr. Reeves's unloaded gun, but dropped it so they could carry the hams and bags of flour they wanted.

Jamie could not move until they found his fiddle case. At that point, Jamie was filled with anger and energy. He jumped up screaming at them, "Leave my fiddle alone!" He kicked them and tried to get hold of the case. They laughed at him and knocked him backwards. Opening the wooden case, and with a shout, they took the fiddle out. Jamie tried again to rescue his fiddle.

The Indians jumped off the boat and beat the fiddle like a drum. Others joined them. They discovered the bow and soon had it broken.

Jamie wanted to jump off the boat, but Mr. Reeves held him back. "We must think only of saving our lives," he cautioned.

Jamie felt helpless and realized Mr. Reeves could do little more. "Oh, Pa, please come and help me. I don't think we can ever reach St. Louis."

Furs to St. Louis

When Mr. Hillis and Mr. Adams reached the top of the cliff, on the side opposite where Teddy had run, they quietly tried to figure the best approach for his rescue. Teddy was guarded by three warriors. He had been stripped of all of his clothing, beaten with sticks, and tied to a tree. Mr. Adams soon realized the three guards were more interested in the hilarity and fun the other warriors were having.

One stuck a big knife into Teddy's face. Another hit his shoulders with sticks, and the third tied a filthy rag over Teddy's mouth. They all gave a hoot and ran to see what all of the laughter and drum sounds were about.

Their distraction gave Mr. Adams and Mr. Hillis a chance to cut the crying, shivering Teddy from the trees where he was tied. They half carried the terrified Teddy down the hill and ran back to Mr. Adam's boat as fast as they could.

Seeing how the warriors were breaking the strings, the bow, and the beautiful red velvet–lined violin case, Jamie yelled as loud as he could, "Stop breaking my violin!" He was going to jump out of the boat to fight for it.

Mr. Reeves pulled him back and shouted, "No, you must not leave the boat, no matter what they do."

The three warriors, who had been left to guard Teddy, joined the others in their fun with the fiddle.

Hoping for help from the other boat, Jamie saw Mr. Adams, Mr. Hillis, and Teddy running from the other side of the hill to Mr. Adam's boat. By pointing and making fast rowing motions, Mr. Adams motioned for Jamie to go midstream as he, Mr. Hillis, and Teddy jumped into Mr. Adams's boat. The two hunters were rowing out before Jamie and Mr. Reeves could get started. Oh, how Jamie hated to leave his fiddle, but more frightening was the thought of being left there.

It was up to Jamie and Mr. Reeves to get started. "I can't do it!" Jamie gasped. "I must do it!" The boat moved a bit, and he was able to thrust the oar down hard and help Mr. Reeves get them moving toward midstream. He was still crying hard over losing his fiddle. "I can't even see, but I'll row as fast as I can anyway," he thought.

The storm was almost over when they made it midstream. They went as fast as they could. Jamie did not dare to look but felt sure that warriors in boats were following them. Even though his clothes were sopping wet from the icy storm, he was so hot, he was sweating all over.

When he felt it was safe, the Long Hunter motioned them to pull up alongside. Jamie saw that Teddy was snuggled in a blanket and didn't even look up. One of the other hunters quickly jumped into Jamie's boat and took over the rowing with Mr. Reeves.

When they stopped to make camp that night, Teddy was dressed in borrowed clothes. Trying to create a peaceful atmosphere when they were unloaded, Mr. Hillis gave Teddy and Jamie each a bucket and asked them to get some water from the nearby spring. Jamie felt he could never laugh again, but the sight of Teddy in those too big and borrowed clothes was so funny, he decided he should walk in front of him; otherwise he might burst out laughing at him.

At the stream, Jamie bent over to fill his bucket. Teddy gave him a hard shove almost knocking him into the water.

Even surprising himself, Jamie swing the bucket around and hit Teddy as hard as he could.

"You knocked the breath out of me! I'll show you, you dumb cockroach! Take that!" Teddy yelled as he punched Jamie on the left jaw.

Jamie knew it was really Teddy's fault that the Indians took his fiddle. "You caused all the trouble, you crazy toad!"

They swung and socked each other as fast and hard as they could. Teddy tripped Jamie. When Jamie fell, he grabbed an ankle and threw Teddy to the ground. There they kicked and punched each other, sometimes one on top and sometimes the other.

Mr. Hillis had come to see what was going on. He sat down and leaned against a tree to watch.

Mr. Reeves had also heard the commotion and came to check.

Jamie wondered what was happening when he felt himself being pulled away from Teddy. After Mr. Reeves had the boys separated, he put his hands on his hips and demanded, "Haven't we had enough trouble for one day!"

Teddy doubled up his fists and shouted, "Jamie started it."

Before Jamie could answer the false accusation, Mr. Reeves said, "I'm not sure I believe you, but I hope he beat you up good!" A motion up the bank caught his eye. Jamie didn't know until then that Mr. Hillis had been watching.

Mr. Reeves said, "Sorry Abe, didn't see you up there. It looked like the boys were hurting each other badly."

"Yes, I agree. Jamie has let the boys push him around too much. He will soon be on his own and must learn to protect himself. For the first time, I believe he can," answered Mr. Hillis. "In St. Louis, he'll have no one to look out for him."

Jamie felt a warm glow to see that Teddy was getting a big bruise on his right eye. Yes, Jamie's eye hurt, and he knew it was swelling. So did other bruises, but it was a good hurt. *It'll be a long time before he shoves me around again*, he thought.

As Jamie washed the mud off of his face in the spring water, he saw his reflection. Not only did the cold water feel good on his bruises, but he was shocked to see how much he looked like his mother. *I wonder if Pa would have been proud of the way I beat up on Teddy.*

After a delicious meal cooked in two big frying pans, the Long Hunter, Mr. Adams, replenished the fire and said he wanted to give some reinforcement to earlier instructions.

"We are all aware of how close we came to being captured by the Indians today. You had all been warned to stay clear of that stretch of shore. The sudden turning of the river tide and the ferocity of the storm forced us into a dangerous area."

"I shall always be grateful to you for saving the life of my son," said Mr. Hillis. "It was very foolish of him to jump out of the boat when he had been told of the danger."

"Yes, we must not have a repeat of such misbehavior," said Mr. Adams. "We lost a lot of good provisions and came near to losing everything, as well as our lives. In the wilderness, men must respect each other, for there may be unknown dangers. Had it not been for the fascination of the Indians with Jamie's fiddle, we would never have been able to rescue Teddy."

All agreed that their brush with the warriors was a close call. They must be careful that they are not in such a dangerous place again, if they can help it.

Mr. Hillis said he wanted to help Jamie get another fiddle. They all wanted to share with Jamie his sad loss by somehow helping him get another violin.

"When Jamie played for little Homer's funeral, I thought an angel had descended from heaven," one of the hunters said.

"Jamie, you must get another violin, for people long to hear beautiful music. You must keep practicing and playing for folks wherever you go," Mr. Adams said.

Mr. Hillis, realizing they would soon be separated from Jamie, felt he should tell them a true story.

All settled themselves comfortably on stumps or logs. One of the hunters added more branches and logs to the fire. Jamie, watching the flames, felt he would fall asleep. He didn't want to miss any of the fireside stories. Each evening the men exchanged stories of narrow escapes, bold encounters with other men and animals, or interesting people they had known. Jamie loved to hear them.

Mr. Hillis began his story. "When I was a lad of around eighteen or so, I fell in love with a beautiful girl. She looked a lot like Mary Beth. We were always partners at square dances and together at parties such as taffy pulls. I asked her to marry me. She said she would have to convince her father before I dared to ask him. I gave her a diamond ring as a token of my love. I hope few young people ever know the grief I knew when she could not marry me."

"What happened? Did she die?" Mr. Adams asked.

"She did much later—so young and beautiful. No, that was not the reason. A new family moved from Arlington to our town, Front Royal, Virginia. They were very well liked by everyone, including me. Their good-looking son started taking my bride-to-be to parties. Her father gave his consent to their marriage." Looking straight at Jamie, he said, "This is about your parents, Jamie."

Startled and unbelieving, Jamie was wide awake. *Could this be true?* he asked himself. *How can this be true? I never heard about it.*

Finally, Jamie realized he heard the croaking of frogs, and the men were all talking together about something else. *I must find out more about my parents*, he thought.

"Mr. Hillis, are you sure that was my mother? I never saw her wear a diamond ring."

"No, you wouldn't have, Jamie, for she insisted I take it back. I did, and I had it made into a tiepin so that I could wear it near my heart."

"Teddy, you may wonder how your mother would feel if she heard this story," added Mr. Hillis.

"Does she know? Is this why you were always worried about Jamie?" Teddy asked.

"Teddy, at this age you probably don't realize what a wonderful mother you have. Yes, she knew Jamie's parents and was very fond of them, too. When his mother died, it was she who said we should help look out for Jamie."

"Is that why you made a crutch for me?" Jamie asked.

"Yes, I guess that is one reason, but, Jamie, I like you for the fine lad you are," Mr. Hillis answered.

Mr. Adams recalled the handsome soldier, Mr. Bacon, who was on his way to St. Louis and camped with him one night.

"It must have been Pa," Jamie said. "Then he surely is somewhere further west from us."

After Jamie went to bed, he had a hard time going to sleep. His mind kept racing over the startling news about his parents. He always thought his mother was pretty, but he never knew she looked something like Mary Beth. Also, it seemed impossible that either of his parents had loved anyone else.

Yes, Teddy's parents had been good to him. Mr. Hillis even went all the way back to Pittsburgh to find him. He bought his carved bird and nest.

Since I beat up on Teddy, I guess I could like him a little, he thought.

Jamie awakened the next morning to the wonderful smell of bacon frying. Mr. Adams said they would stay in an inn the next night. Travel on the river was more fun. Jamie learned to see where animals had made well-trodden paths down to the river. Through a tangle of leaves, he even saw the eyes of a raccoon.

The landscape changed as they approached Cairo, Illinois, and continued on to the Great Mississippi River. They finally arrived in St. Louis. Jamie was sure he would see Pa on shore, but he did not.

Mr. Reeves helped Jamie find a place to work and live. His job was in a general store where he also had a room. He often went home with Mr. Beaudell, the store owner, and ate with his family.

Mr Beaudell suggested, "Jamie, how about putting your President Washington oil painting in the store window? People out here have a very high regard for him. It might draw customers into the store."

"All right," answered Jamie. "I'd like people to see it."

The day came for his Virginia and Ohio friends to leave him. It was sad, but he knew he might someday see them again. He was most excited about Mr. Adams saying he was pretty sure he would be bringing his bride, Grandma Nelson, to St. Louis real soon. She would then be Mrs. Adams.

On Sundays and evenings Jamie would wander about town looking for his Pa. At such times he was reminded of his scary experience in Pittsburgh. He stayed away from dirty, sneaky-looking people. He asked many folks about his pa, but he never found any who thought they had seen him.

One morning Mr. Beaudell asked, "Jamie, how about you keeping the store for a while today? Mrs. Beaudell wants me to help her. Many friends are coming to our house to make apple butter."

"Yes, Mr. Beaudell, I think I know the prices real well, and I know where you keep things. I'd be glad to take care of the store," Jamie said with confidence. "Besides, there have not been very many people in to trade today."

"Fine, Jamie, I feel you have a good understanding of what needs to be done, so I'll leave you in charge. I'll see you later this afternoon. Mrs. Beaudell expects you to eat with us this evening. I'll see you in a while," he called over his shoulder as he went out the front door.

Already there were leaves falling, and they were being tracked into the store. Jamie decided to sweep up the floor. He was just finishing when there were several unusually loud gun shots.

People started running toward the river. He started out the door and remembered he was in charge of the store.

Mr. Carver, from the livery, came running by and said, "Come on, Jamie, it's a big boat that has just arrived."

Jamie did not dare to leave the store. He watched as many people ran toward the river. Could Pa be on that boat? Jamie did not know whether it came from the east or the west. So many times he had been disappointed when boats had arrived and Pa was not there.

People started coming into the store so fast Jamie could not take care of them all. They were excited about the new arrivals and didn't seem to mind waiting for him. Fortunately, Mr. Beaudell returned. There was much talk about the big boat and its passengers. Mr. Beaudell said he would put a ring on the calendar for that day of September 26, 1806.

Several of the soldiers from the boat had families in St. Louis and were already dismissed from their duty. Others remained on guard duty.

"Jamie, it very well could be that someone who came in today may know your pa. When we take care of this rush of people coming in to trade, we can go and find out." Jamie sure didn't want to wait, but they had to take care of their customers. He was very busily filling a small bag of sugar in the back of the store. He thought he heard a voice that sounded like his pa's. "Could it, can it be?" he asked himself. "Oh, I've

been so disappointed so many times, I'm not even going to look at whoever is talking like him. I'll find out when we go to see the boat,"

The voice that sounded like Pa's was saying, "Sir, would you mind telling me where you came upon the oil painting of George Washington, which you have in the window?"

Jamie could contain himself no longer. He looked up and saw that the man had a beard. It couldn't be Pa.

"Jamie, would you want to tell this man about the oil painting?" Mr. Beaudell called to Jamie.

When Jamie looked into the face of the man who had asked about the painting, he looked right into the deep blue eyes of his pa. The sugar scoop fell with a loud clatter.

They ran into each others arms.

Held in the safe, strong arms of his pa at last, Jamie felt tears running down his cheeks. When his father released him, he took hold of his shoulders and said, "Oh, Jamie, I've found you."

Jamie saw his pa had tears in his eyes as he said, "My very own son, how you have grown. Now, you even look more like your dear mother."

"Pa, did you know?"

Once again he pulled Jamie into his arms where he held him tight for a moment and said nothing. He then almost whispered, "President Jefferson sent me word through the army. I felt I could not live without her." Releasing Jamie and looking him straight in the eye he continued, "As the weeks passed, I knew I had to face reality. You have no grandparents and only one parent. Don't worry, Jamie, I will not go away again without you."

"All I want is to be with you. Where have you been?"

"I was assigned by President Jefferson as a guard to go with Meriwether Lewis and William Clark. We explored not only the Louisiana territory but far beyond it. We were to map rivers and to seek new supply routes and outlets for American fur trappers and traders. They made maps and records of what lay in this vast and beautiful land."

"Just this morning, there were a couple of men in the store talking about the return of a party who had been all the way out to the Pacific Ocean," Jamie said.

"This is the one. The expedition had been kept a secret by President Jefferson. It has caused much excitement. I had to stay on board when we first arrived, on guard duty."

"And I had to stay on duty here in the store when your boat came in," said Jamie.

"There is so much to tell you," said Jamie's father. "First of all, the reason I came into the store was because I wondered how the picture of Washington could be here in St. Louis. It certainly looked like the one your grandfather traded for his horse. Did you bring it from home?"

"Yes, I did, for Mother had made me promise to take good care of it. Now, how glad I am that it brought you into the store," Jamie answered.

"My boy, west of us there are mountains so tall they have snow on them all year. Plains are so big, the human eye cannot see the end of them."

"Pa, do you think we could go see this great land in the west?" asked Jamie.

"For sure, son, we'll go together on this adventure."